Editorial Briefs

I know this is the page where I usually give you a preview of what's coming in this issue, but my attention has been somewhat scattered as of late and I'd rather spend the time in this column talking about heroes. We've all had one at some point in our lives, otherwise you wouldn't be reading this issue and I wouldn't be writing this column. They've come from all walks of life and genres including, but certainly not limited to, Entertainment, Sports, Music, History, Politics, the Armed Forces, and so many more. In some cases, they've even been found in our own homes.

Do you remember the first time you held a signature that you'd been wanting in your hands? The excitement. The feel of the blood rushing to your fingers as a smile makes its way across your face. I've had that feeling quite a few times, but I've found it to be the most enjoyable when there's someone there to share the enthusiasm with me. Someone who knows the joy that I'm experiencing not only because they love me and know my love of collecting, but because they too have had the same experience at a point in their life and are now reliving that cherished moment as they watch mine unfold.

With the untimely deaths of so many of our beloved actors, musicians, singers, sports players, and historical figures, I find myself spending more and more time reflecting on the heroes of childhood and those my parents grew up with. When you're watching an episode of a television show you used to love when you were younger, it rarely occurs to you while you're relishing in that moment of your youth that those people are now 20, 30, or 40 years older. You can't imagine the day you'll pick up the paper, turn on the television, or open your homepage and see that one of those favorites is now gone. It makes it even worse when the realization hits that nobody lives forever, but why is it that no matter who it is that goes next it's always one of the really good ones? Don't get me wrong, I'm certainly not trying to discount anyone's acting career or life as being less important than someone else's, but have you ever noticed that when one legend goes two more are soon to follow? So by the time all of us grow up, who's left to be our heroes?

I guess it's all a matter of putting people on pedestals. I should know. My parents put me on one from the day I was born and I'm not sure if I've ever stepped down from it since. In all actuality, they're the real heroes in the picture. In fact, it's them that have given all of us the freedom to go our own way, do what we love, and embrace us for what we are and who we've become. So if you've not done so lately, take a moment to thank your parents for encouraging you to reach for what you wanted out of life, whether they're physically with you or not, because I guarantee they'd remember the smile on your face when you held that first autograph.

This issue is dedicated to A.Y. Altman, who shared his love of collecting with his son, who has in turn shared his writing talents and autograph collection with the readers of Autograph Quarterly for the past two issues. As you read the article Rich has prepared for this issue, you'll completely understand why.

Until next time... Victoria

The Publisher's View

Welcome to another edition of Autograph Quarterly: the only in-print magazine to serve the hobby/trade today. As usual, we are very proud of the content of this current issue and hope you will enjoy it too.

We don't publish fluff, but instead give you information you can use and file away as reference. In fact, most of our subscribers tell us they wouldn't dream of throwing out and issue due to its incredible and useful content.

That's by design. We work hard to bring balanced (sports, entertainment, historical etc) articles that are meaty. We know you don't want to read about some guy talking about his own inventory or how he obtained a single autograph or get lists of addresses that will only yield secretarial responses. Instead we give you useful research by the world's top experts and collectors with very few ads to clutter it up. This magazine has always been a labor of love for me and will continue to be one hopefully for years to come.

We are excited that in these pages we have given our first ten Autograph Quarterly awards for Authentic merchandise dealers on eBay! eBay, of course, is the largest source of forged material offered daily in the world today and always has been. They show a blatant disregard for this since they disbanded their own fraud department as it related to autographs, and we all know the frustration of "reporting" bad material only to see it still listed. This is because appparetnly they rarely pull things down unless someone has paid a third party company a fee to get an "opinion" on the item, which is a clear sign that everyone should remember eBay is a business and in the business to make money - nothing else.

eBay's policies to their sellers have become almost dictatorial in nature with absurd requirements like their newest one that all dealers who want to qualify for their top awards and discounts must ship for free and must ship within 24 hours! Of course you must also use Paypal (their company) to do all of this, and their fees to list are so high now that most of the best autograph dealers in the world have stopped selling on their site. Christophe Stickel, Charles Searle, Todd Mueller, Walter Burks, Piece of the Past, and dozens more have stopped altogether preferring their own web sites for sales.

It is due to all of this mess that Autograph Quarterly decided to bestow a Autograph Quarterly Good Dealer award in our pages to those eBay sellers who consistently have shown our panel of experts that they are selling predominently real items, who also stand behind their items, have contact information listed for them, and have been in business longer than 15 minutes.

Here's how the program works. A panel of known autograph experts in several fields from entertainment to historical, presidential to sports, each vetted the dealers' online inventories for a period of weeks of assorted offerings on eBay to determine if the majority (if not all) of their items passed authenticity tests, and if so, if additionally it was easy to reach these dealers. In other words, whether the dealers posted their phone numbers and addresses, not just a P.O. Box, etc... How long they have been operating as a dealer in autographed materials and whether they offerred their own Certificate of Authenticity. Not an opinion service but their own COA, and then backed up their COA with transeferable lifetime guarantees of authenticity.

If all of these pieces of criteria have been met, then Autograph Quarterly proudly adds the online dealer's name to the exclusive list of dealers we think our readers may safely enjoy collecting autographed pieces from. On the back cover, you will see the eBay seller names of our first ten dealers who meet all of our strict criteria. Congratulations to them for making the cut!

We are not warranting if these dealers' prices are in line with reality. That isn't a decision for us to make. We only believe that they are safe and reputable to deal with and may therefore display our seal of approval with pride.

Lastly, we will continue to vette. Our experts will inspect the products the dealers list in the future and if at any time we feel they no longer qualify as reputable members of the Autograph Quarterly Dealer Seal of Approval program, we will ask them to relinquish the seal in all advertising, and we will remove them from our published and online lists as well as notify our readers of our decision to do so and why we took that step.

Until next time!
Samuel Xidas

Richard MacCallum

~ Chicago ~

Fine Autographs Since 1972

~ London ~

866 Auburn Court • Highland Park, Illinois 60035
(847) 432-7942 Phone • (847) 432-8685 Fax 24 Hours
0798-922-0386 • London, England

The Autographs: The following presentations are vintage signatures that in most cases have been removed from old autograph albums, letters, documents, etc. and have been mounted under a photograph. Most photos used are approximately 8x10 in size. They are double matted most often in black and white, or other colors that work best with that style of photograph. Most photos are black and white. Most overall sizes are approximately 12x17. Snapshots of these pieces, as well as photocopies of the signatures are available. I carry signatures from all areas of history (and have so since 1972). The items listed below are other autographs available. Some are matted with a photo, some are signed photos, and some are just signatures only.
Call for more details. Foreign orders always welcome.

Walt Disney - $1,495.00

Cary Grant - $295.00

Marilyn Monroe & Joe DiMaggio - $2,995.00

Walt Disney - $1,495.00
Marlene Dietrich - $195.00
"Houdini" - $795.00
Douglas Fairbanks Sr. - $250.00
Cecil B. DeMille - $195.00
Mother Teresa - $425.00
Henry Fonda - $250.00
Jimi Hendrix - $1,495.00
George Burns - $125.00
George Reeves - $695.00
Colin Clive - $595.00
Liberace (with Piano
    Drawing) - $295.00
Buddy Holly - $795.00
Lupe Velez - $225.00
Margaret Hamilton - $250.00
"Dr. Seuss" (Theodor Seuss
    Geisel) - $395.00
Rockey Marciano - $450.00
Marilyn Monroe - $2,495.00
Frank Lloyd Wright - $595.00
"Laurel & Hardy" - $895.00
Helen Hayes - $125.00
Michael Jackson - $325.00
Lon Chaney Sr. - $795.00
Clark Gable & Vivien
    Leigh - $595.00
Amelia Earhart - $625.00
Ernest Hemingway - $3,150.00
Edward G. Robinson - $250.00
Carole Lombard - $275.00
"The Blues Brothers" - $495.00
Grace Kelly - $395.00
The "Apollo XI Crew" - $2,595.00
U.S. Grant - $595.00
Basil Rathbone - $295.00
Mary Astor - $250.00
Geronimo - $8,595.00
Gary Cooper - $250.00
Cary Grant - $295.00
Casey Stengel - $495.00
W.C. Fields - $395.00
Jimmy Stewart &
    Donna Reed - $325.00
Jimmy Stewart - $125.00
Jimmy Stewart &
    June Allyson - $195.00
Jimmy Stewart &
    Maureen O'Hara - $195.00
Jimmy Stewart &
    Frank Capra - $295.00
Jimmy Stewart &
    Marlene Dietrich - $350.00

James Dean - $2,295.00
"The Maltese Falcon" - $2,195.00
Steve McQueen - $695.00
Sigmund Freud - $1,295.00
Martin Luther King Jr. -
    $2,195.00
"The Wizard of Oz" - $2,195.00
Oscar Wilde - $995.00
Judy Garland - $395.00
Frederic Remington - $525.00
Charles M. Russell - $495.00
James Dean & Sal Mineo
    (on same page) - $2,995.00
Natalie Wood - $295.00
Frank Sinatra - $395.00
Gerald R. Ford - $295.00
Maxfield Parish - $295.00
Alberto Vargas - $425.00
Salvador Dali - $395.00
Erte - $250.00
Marc Chagall - $450.00
Andy Warhol - $425.00
Katharine Hepburn - $275.00
Alfred Hitchcock - $895.00
Rita Hayworth - $225.00
Edgar Allan Poe - $7,995.00
Harold Lloyd - $325.00
Will Rogers - $595.00
Wiley Post - $250.00
Lech Walesa - $295.00
Mary Pickford - $225.00
Charles A. Comiskey - $650.00
John, Lionel & Ethel
    Barrymore - $595.00
John Phillip Sousa - $350.00
Samual Goldwyn - $225.00
Louis B. Mayer - $250.00
Eddie "Rochester"
    Anderson - $195.00
Kurt Vonnegut - $150.00
Marilyn Monroe &
    Joe DiMaggio - $2,995.00
Claudette Colbert - $150.00
"The DiMaggio
    Brothers" - $1,295.00
Clayton Moore - $125.00
Eubie Blake - $150.00
Joe DiMaggio (Signed
    Baseball) - $695.00
Ted Williams (Signed
    Baseball) - $595.00
Mickey Mantle (Signed
    Baseball) - $695.00

Mark Twain - $1,195.00
Walter Huston - $175.00
Ty Cobb - $795.00
Charles Laughton - $195.00
Hal Roach - $195.00
"Gilligan's Island" Cast
    Photo (All 7) - $695.00
Spencer Tracy - $275.00
Jim Morrison - $695.00
Jerry Garcia - $295.00
Ronald Reagan - $395.00
Connie Mack - $695.00
Duke Ellington - $295.00
James Cagney - $175.00
James Cagney &
    Corinne Calvet - $225.00
Bud Abbott & Lou
    Costello - $695.00
Tallulah Bankhead - $175.00
Brigitte Bardot - $125.00
Enrico Caruso - $275.00
Lillian Gish - $125.00
Alger Hiss - $295.00
Bela Lugosi - $595.00
Truman Capote - $225.00
"The Marx Brothers" - $1,395.00
Fay Wray - $175.00
"The Three Stooges" Moe,
    Curley (first names), Larry
    (full name) - $1,495.00
Lucille Ball & Desi Arnaz
    (Full Names) - $595.00
Menachem Begin - $395.00
Yul Brynner - $195.00
Shirley Temple - $295.00
Charles Bronson - $150.00
Madonna (Nude) - $275.00
Margaret Thatcher - $295.00
Peter Lorre - $275.00
Muhammad Ali - $225.00
Roland Winters "Charlie
    Chan" - $125.00
Fred Astaire &
    Ginger Rogers - $395.00
Ronald Coleman - $175.00
Eric Clapton - $75.00
Linus Pauling - $175.00
Humphrey Bogart - $695.00
Boris Karloff - $2,250.00
"Father Knows Best" Cast
    Photo (all 5) - $495.00
Buck Jones - $295.00
John F. Kennedy - $1,895.00

James Dean - $2,295.00

Buddy Holly - $795.00

Lucille Ball & Desi Arnaz - $595.00

Boris Karloff - $2,250.00

John Wayne - $1,195.00

"The DiMaggio Brothers"
Vince - Joe - Dom - $1,295.00

Muhammad Ali (1963) - $225.00

Ernest Hemingway - $3,150.00

~ WE DO NOT HAVE A WEB SITE, OR AN E-MAIL ADDRESS. ONLY ONE-ON-ONE PERSONALIZED SERVICE. ~

Stephen Koschal
Autographs, Signed Books, Authentications

Established in 1967, we have supplied libraries, universities, museums, collectors and dealers worldwide. We have been one of the leading advocates of autograph education and are responsible for creating and maintaining possibly the largest autograph reference library in the hobby. We pioneered the establishment of the first fourteen autograph educational courses, of which we instructed two of them.

Our educational writings on the subject of autograph collecting can be found in every autograph trade publication as well as the publications of every major autograph organization.

We offer only genuine autographs in all fields of collecting and in all price ranges.

Our reference books are sought by all those who have an interest in education themselves on collecting autographs. Reference books available, shipping additional:

Gerald R. Ford Autograph Study by Stephen Koschal...$7.50

Robert F. Kennedy Autograph Study by TerMolin, Keyes, Koschal...$20.00

Tiger Woods Signature Study by Stephen Koschal and Todd Mueller..$1.95

Thomas Jefferson's Invisible Hand by Stephen Koschal and Andreas Wiemer...........................$10.00

The Collector's Guide to Muhammad Ali Autographs by Shawn Anderson, Markus Brandes, and Stephen Koschal...$15.00

Ronald Reagan and Nelle Reagan Autograph Mystery Uncovered by Patricia Claren, Stephen Koschal, and Ron Werntz..$10.00

The History of Collecting Executive Mansion, White House, and The White House Cards Signed by the Presidents and their First Ladies by Lynne E. Keyes and Stephen Koschal........................$20.00

Presidents of the United States Autopen Guide by Stephen Koschal and Andreas Wiemer........$15.00

Stephen Koschal's authentication service is utilized by collectors worldwide, and by dealers, auction houses, and by other authentication services.   Occasional catalogs issued.

ACTIVELY PURCHASING AUTOGRAPH COLLECTIONS
Immediate Payment

Stephen Koschal
P.O. Box 311061
Miami, FL 33231 USA

Phone: 561-315-3622
E-Mail: skoschal@aol.com
Website: www.stephenkoschal.com

Experience the Difference Authenticity Makes!

   Piece of the Past, Inc. is pleased to announce the official launch of its new online auction site! Housed at www.pieceofthepast.com, this site replaces most, if not all, of our eBay sales activity as well as our monthly catalogs.

   You may be wondering why we'd make this move. The answer is simple. We want our customers to have the very best experience when adding to their autograph and/or memorabilia collections, and by controlling all of the aspects of the auction process, you're guaranteed to receive the best service at always fair prices.

   The site is up and running right now with an array of fabulous photos, costumes, and props, so the follow the directions below and join us now. You won't be disappointed!

Registration Instructions

1 - Go to http://www.pieceofthepast.com

2 - Click the button that says CLICK HERE TO REGISTER

3 - Enter your name, address, phone number, and other information

4 - You will receive an e-mail confirming your registration and assigning
a bidder number. That is your permanent number.

5 - Log into your account and start shopping!

6 - Check back often because we'll be listing roughly 200 items per week.

9030 West Sahara Avenue, Suite 448 - Las Vegas, NV 89117 - (888) 689-7079

INSIDE THIS ISSUE

CHECK THE BACK COVER TO SEE WHO MADE THE CUT!

Autograph Dealer
Seal of Approval

Selected as an eBay
dealer you can trust by
the Autograph Quarterly
Team of Experts

2012

Autograph Quarterly

Publisher
S. Eugene Xidas

Editor-in-Chief
Victoria Gregory

Editorial Assistant
Christine McDermott

Contributors
Richard E. Altman, Stephen Koschal, Dr. Marian Zoltan,
Patricia Claren, Mark Gross, and Brian Green

Questions about Autograph Quarterly?
questions@autographquarterly.com

Autograph Quarterly welcomes collecting enthusiasts and
dealers alike to submit articles for inclusion in upcoming
issues. If you'd like to have an article considered, please
e-mail it to either the publisher or editor. If you'd prefer to
mail in your submission, or if you have a book on the hobby
you'd like to have reviewed, please send it to the address
listed below. We will contact you to let you know if your
submission has been accepted for publication.

Please note that all articles submitted become the property
of Autograph Quarterly and cannot be released for inclusion
in any other publication.

Advertising inquiries should be directed to Victoria Gregory.

victoriagregory@autographquarterly.com

Single copies are available for purchase through Amazon.com

Autograph Quarterly Magazine
119 Hickory Street
Henderson, NV 89015

www.autographquarterly.com

Take Me Out to the Ballgame...
By Richard E. Altman

I'm a second-generation autograph collector. What makes this meaningful is that it gives me something extra in common with my Dad, something I came to on my own. Only later did I learn that I shared this seemingly frivolous hobby with the steadiest person I knew.

For me, acquiring the autograph, whether in person, by mail or by outright purchase is my futile attempt to own a piece of history; to account for a moment in time –however brief—in the life of a significant life. I collect what I like, even if what I like is significant or collectible to few people other than me. In short, it makes for a very eclectic assemblage. Sports, movies and TV, the literary world and the art world, history and politics, standup comedy and music all have places in my autograph archives.

For my father, growing up in the Bronx meant that the local celebrities were the New York Yankees. Oh sure, there was the time in November, 1935 when Detroit Tiger legend and James Monroe High School alum (class of '29) Hank Greenberg paid a visit to Morris High School in the Bronx –where my Dad toiled as an earnest Freshman -- and signed an autograph for him. "Hammerin' Hank" (Greenberg held that moniker decades before Hank Aaron was bequeathed it) even inscribed it *"To my friend Arthur with best wishes."*

Hank Greenburg, Detroit Tigers Star First Baseman

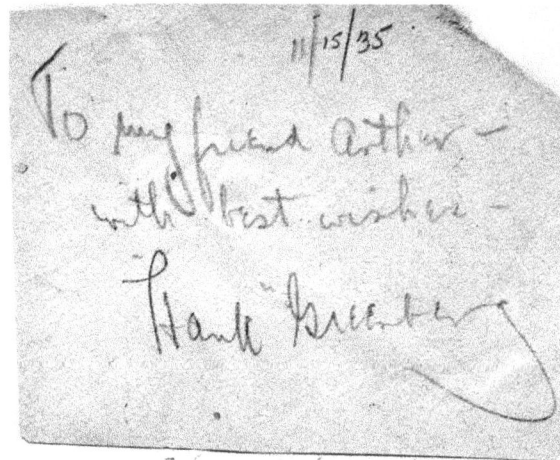

Hank Greenburg Autograph, Bronx, NY
November 1935

And there were some "track and field champs" whose signatures young Arthur acquired during his senior year at Monroe: Glenn Cunningham, Archie San Romani and Harold Lamb. Though those names may not be instantly recognizable today, a quick trip to Google will lay out an impressive set of running records and an inspiring set of personal histories and extraordinary triumphs.

But it is vintage Yankee World Series baseball, specifically the 1936 subway series between the Bronx Bombers and their Manhattan rivals, the New York Giants on which we hang this tale of intrepid autograph collecting.

The Yankees had been going through a dry spell…their last appearance in a World Series had been the 1932 victory over the Chicago Cubs which was notable for far more than simply notching the teams' fourth World Series championship. (How quaint and approachable that sounds compared with the 27 World Championships presently held by the Yanks). Still, the '32 series was the thing that baseball myths and legends are built on, *even if it actually happened the way popular history tells it.*

Here was the moment when the great Babe Ruth – his bat still resting on his left shoulder – extended his right arm towards the centerfield stands of Wrigley Field and then proceeded to pound the very next pitch into that "called" location in the seats. Detractors argue that he was pointing at something, not calling his shot but this moment of on-field heroics so captured the imagination that it remains to many if not most baseball fans the single most iconic event in the history of the sport.

Mega heroics or not, age and over-indulgence caught up with the Bambino and he unceremoniously departed the Yankees after the 1934 season, following two pennantless years. The 1935 season without Ruth faired no better.

Arthur Altman, Bronx NY, Age 16, 1936

So it was on this October day in 1936 that a boy of 16 legged it from his home on College Avenue and East 169th Street in the Bronx the mile or so to Yankee Stadium at 161st Street and River Avenue. Even though the Stadium was right next to the "EL" – New York's elevated train line, the nickel fare could be better put towards a hotdog at the game than on a short hop in an aboveground subway car. Besides, the autumn weather was fair and in the 40s, making a brisk jaunt through Bronx streets a mere walk in the urban park. The route took him up 169th Street, passed the Mom & Pop shops like the butcher and the chicken flicker (who could render a recently departed bird bare of pesky pinfeathers in a blur of activity) or the glazer who also patched window screens when the stifling New York summer demanded a breeze be let inside and the bugs be kept outside. *No AC back in the day...* As 169th Street met up with the Grand Concourse, the tone of walk changed. Mom & Pop shops gave way to chain stores like Woolworth's. The Grand Concourse was the Bronx' answer to the Champs-Élysées. No jarring cobblestone streets here like elsewhere in the Bronx. The wide Grand Concourse roadway was paved smoothly in asphalt.

The walk was nothing new for Arthur. He had made the trek many times – not to go to the Stadium – but to deliver hand laundered shirts from Chin Lee's Chinese Laundry on 169th Street to a discerning resident of the ultra luxurious Concourse Plaza Hotel across from the Stadium and the newly built Bronx Borough Hall (a project of FDR's WPA program).

Following a reported six-hour rain delay, the opening game of the '36 series was played on September 30th at the Polo Grounds in Manhattan, the Giant's home field. With President Franklin Roosevelt watching, the Giants gave the soggy Yanks a 6-1 drubbing. Stung by the embarrassing and ignoble defeat, the Bombers came back the very next day. In game two –still at the Polo Grounds and with FDR in attendance again – the Yanks devastated the Giants by the score of 18-4. That game remains the highest scoring World Series game by a single team. (The highest combined score honors goes to the '93 Toronto Blue Jays 15-14 victory over the Philadelphia Phillies).

Front Cover of the 1936 World Series Program

Game three of the '36 series moved to the Bronx and since no days off for travel were needed, the series bumped along seamlessly from the Polo Grounds to "the House that

Ruth Built." Besides the Yankees second victory of the series – a modest 2-1 affair with one of the winning runs coming courtesy of a solo homer by Lou Gehrig – the games most memorable moment for Arthur came when a dapper gent sitting a few rows in front of him in the bleachers, held up his straw boater hat to catch a fly ball. The ball of course crashed through the skimmer's crown and the now slightly less dapper gent was sadly, sans ball and once stylish lid.

New York Yankees Owner Jake Ruppert, photographed in the stands circa 1920s – Image courtesy of the National Baseball Hall of Fame Library, Cooperstown, NY

"The Mayor of Harlem" legendary dancer and mega-movie star of the day Bill "Bojangles" Robinson. A die-hard Yankee fan and close friend of Lou Gehrig and later, Joe DiMaggio

Bob "Suitcase" Seeds only played for the Yankees during the 1936 series, but it was enough to earn him a World Series Ring and a place in history for something other than his much traded and traveled career.

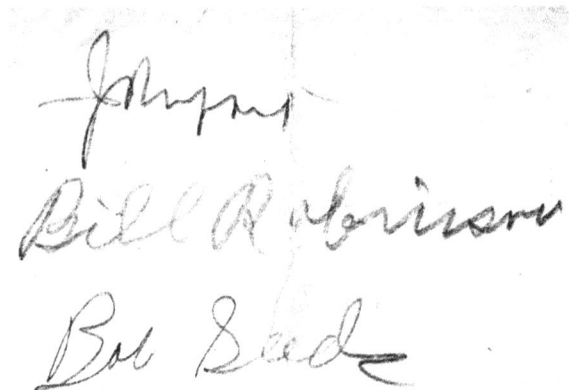

Autographs of Jake Ruppert, Bill Robinson and Bob Seeds obtained at Yankee Stadium by Arthur at the third game of 1936 World Series.

At the game's conclusion, some fans filtered out on to the street through the closest exits, while others took a short cut across the field to reach a more convenient egress. Spotting a discarded program, Arthur picked it up and headed across the field where Yankees Owner Jake Ruppert was still sitting in his box with mega movie star and tap-dancing legend Bill "Bojangles" Robinson. Known as the honorary "Mayor of Harlem" and a die-hard Yankees fan, Bojangles was a well-known and welcome VIP figure at the Stadium, despite the fact that the Major Leagues would not be integrated until Jackie Robinson donned Dodger Blue eleven years later. The Yankees – to their eternal shame – did not integrate until Elston Howard joined the team in 1955.

Following Arthur's rewarding encounter with Ruppert and Robinson, he noticed a Giants batboy gathering up soiled towels from the visitors' dugout and carrying them into the clubhouse. Calling out to him, "can I help?" and hearing no objection, our enterprising young hero gathered up a mess of towels and proceeded into the clubhouse area under the stands, where he found himself at the very crossroads of the baseball world. In those days – in fact until 1946 – the Yankees dugout was on the third base line, not the first base line as it is today. Nonetheless, once underneath the stands, the visitor's clubhouse was at the base of the stairs, directly underneath the Yankee's Clubhouse. The visitors would have to walk to their dugout in a tunnel running under the stands.

Former New York Yankees PR Director Marty Appel sets the scene:

"The original Yankee clubhouse, on the third base side, was up a flight of wooden stairs. Inside were real metal "lockers" – they had doors that locked! – not the stalls that simply borrow the word "locker" today. And the uniforms of Babe Ruth (#3) and Lou Gehrig (#4) remained in their lockers after their retirements, with clubhouse man Pete Sheehy an early proponent of all things ceremonial and honorary. (In 1976, the clubhouse was named after Pete)..."

It was in that tunnel/corridor, having deposited his cache of dirty towels (presumably in some suitable receptacle) that Arthur, pencil and scavenged World Series program in hand, embarked on a mission to collect autographs from the victorious Yankee players.

Team Picture of the World Champion 1936 New York Yankees. Image courtesy of the National Baseball Hall of Fame Library, Cooperstown, NY

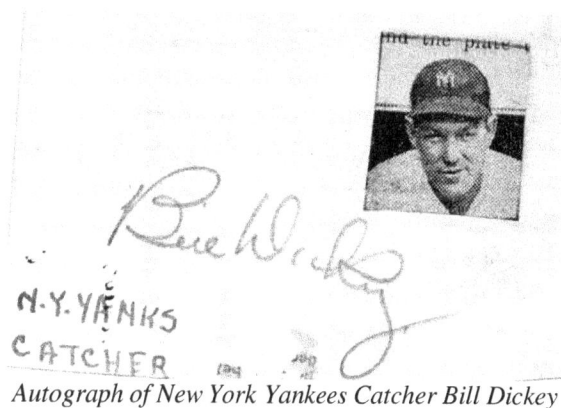

Autograph of New York Yankees Catcher Bill Dickey

THREE HALL OF FAME YANKEES: The legendary "Iron Horse," first baseman Lou Gehrig is flanked by up-and coming superstar, centerfielder Joe DiMaggio (R) and Bill Dickey, the catcher who made "Number 8" great before Yogi Berra further enhanced that number's cache. The Yanks retired the number for both Berra and Dickey in 1972. Image courtesy of the National Baseball Hall of Fame Library, Cooperstown, NY.

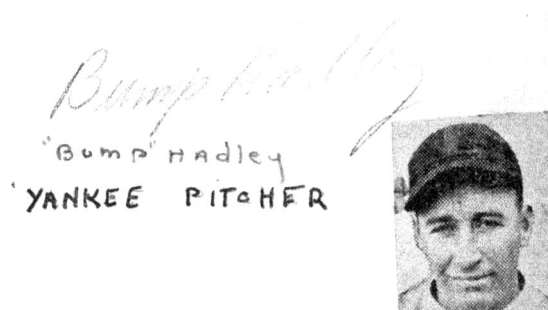

Autograph of Bump Hadley, obtained following game three of the 1936 World Series at Yankee Stadium

Irving "Bump" Hadley, the Yankee's winning pitcher in game three of the '36 series

Autograph of Earle Combs, obtained following game three of the 1936 World Series at Yankee Stadium

Earle Combs, a member of the Yankee's 1927 "Murderer's Row" lineup played center field and was that team's lead-off hitter. Combs was one of six players from the '27 team to be inducted into the Baseball Hall of Fame. He spent his entire baseball career with the New York Yankees and was a coach on the 1936 team.

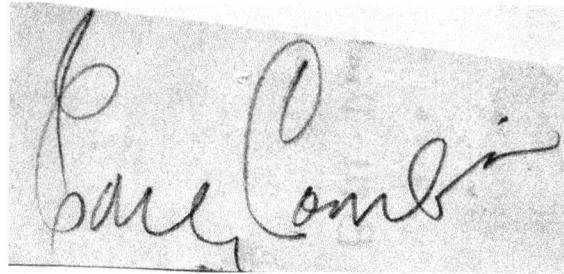

Autograph of Monte Pearson, obtained following game three of the 1936 World Series at Yankee Stadium

Yankee pitcher Monte Pearson pitched for the Yankees on the '36, '37, '38 and '39 World Series winning teams, posting a 4-0 record (three complete games and one shutout) and an astounding 1.01 ERA. Pearson also has the distinction of pitching the first no-hitter in Yankee Stadium history (versus Cleveland during the '38 regular season).

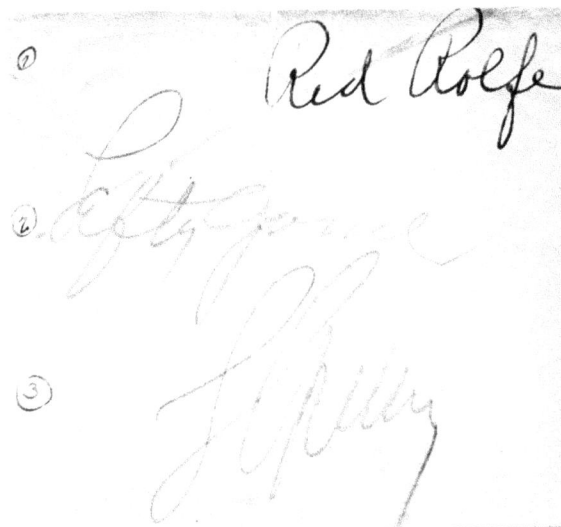

Autographs of three Yankee greats: third baseman Red Rolfe, southpaw pitcher Lefty Gomez and iconic "Iron Horse" first baseman Lou Gehrig, obtained following game three of the 1936 World Series at Yankee Stadium

Yankee Third Baseman Red Rolfe

Yankee Southpaw Pitcher Lefty Gomez

The autographs came fast in the post-game pandemonium. Outfielder Bob "Suitcase" Seeds (so nicknamed because of his much traveled and traded major league career (five teams in ten years) signed just below owner Ruppert and Bill Robinson on the program. Catcher Bill Dickey (whose number 8 was retired in 1972 when the team retired catcher Yogi Berra's number 8), the day's winning pitcher Bump Hadley, coach and former career Yankee Earle Combs, pitcher Monte Pearson while Red Rolfe, Lefty Gomez and Lou Gehrig's signatures were stacked in that order, with Rolfe's the only one in ink. And oh yeah, a promising young rookie named Joe DiMaggio -- late of the Pacific Coast League -- obliged the 16 year old with his signature as well.

Alas, moving homes in the course of putting this piece together caused the rookie DiMaggio signature to become temporarily misfiled and I am unable put my hands on it by press time. *Mea Culpa.*

MIGHTY YOUNG JOE: His callow look notwithstanding, this is the frozen form of the one and only "Yankee Clipper," Joltin' Joe DiMaggio, early in his pinstripe career.
Image courtesy of the National Baseball Hall of Fame Library, Cooperstown, NY.

Arthur turned to the Giant's area and managed to score the signature of Fred Fitzsimmons (that day's losing pitcher) on the program.

Autograph of New York Giants pitcher Fred Fitzsimmons, signed at Yankee Stadium following his loss to the Yankees in game three of the '36 World Series.

New York Giants right-handed pitcher Fred Fitzsimmons, who lost game three of the 1936 World Series to the New York Yankees.

Pushing his luck he then approached the usually genial Giant slugger Mel Ott. It is said that when Leo Durocher uttered the famous words, "nice guys finish last" he was referring to Mel Ott. One guesses that the day's loss put him in an uncharacteristically unfriendly humor, particularly when confronted by a likely Yankee fan asking for an autograph. Ott's response was short and to the point:

"Get outta here."

And so, recognizing that acquiescing to Ott's orders was the better part of valor and with his treasure securely in hand, the 16 year-old Arthur departed through the dugout as he had entered, trooped home to a 169th street and College Avenue and promptly did the predictable...*and the unthinkable.*

Yes fellow autographistas, he cut all of the signatures out of the program, mounted them onto individual 3" x 5" cards and discarded the program remnants. *I'll wait a moment for the screams of anguish to subside.*

For the record, the Yankees won the '36 World Series four games to two and proceeded to dominate the fall classic with back-to-back-to back wins in '37, '38 and '39.

***

There are things that happen in baseball. Legendary things...that are so engrained in our collective consciousness that only a couple of words are needed to recall them with no further explanation required. "The called shot." "The Speech" and the "the streak" are three such moments. Their protagonists – Ruth, Gehrig and DiMaggio – loom large in Yankee, and by extension, baseball lore. "The speech" came July 4th, 1939 and is forever remembered for the words uttered by a dying man to his teammates and his loyal fans. *"Today I consider myself the luckiest man on the face of the earth"*

The man of course, was the Yankee's own Iron Horse, Lou Gehrig. Nearly two years later the disease that bears his name, took his life. When Gehrig breathed his last on June 2nd 1941 he was seventeen days shy of his 38th birthday and "the streak," the third iconic event of this set was only 19-games long, and not yet considered all that iconic. Nonetheless, these were the nascent days of Joe DiMaggio's still unmatched 56-consecutive game hitting binge that began on May 15th 1941. DiMaggio would not "go 0-fer" again until July16th.

During that streak the imagination of the American public was captured and held hostage. Hit songs chronicling Joe D's exploits were playing on the radio; Bill Robinson even tap-danced on top of the Yankee's dugout in celebration. But it was another moment...one that the venerable New York Times merely mentioned in its coverage of Lou Gehrig's passing that stands out for its time.

Despite the crowds of mourning fans and admirers outside of the Church where Lou Gehrig's funeral service was conducted, the invitation only crowd inside was so private and intimate that scarcely half the seats were filled. Among those invited and designated as honorary pallbearers for the Yankee's fallen "Iron Horse." were Yankee manager Joe McCarthy, Gehrig's roommate, Bill Dickey and once again, Bill "Bojangles" Robinson.

***

Following his graduation from Morris High School in 1938, Arthur took the overland bus west to Southern California to visit a boyhood friend from the Bronx who had relocated there with his family a few years earlier. Taking a room near the LaBrea Tar Pits, Arthur continued his pursuit of the celebrated signature and acquired an impressive array of stars of the day. One such star was Gary Cooper, who in 1942 starred as Lou Gehrig in the classic baseball biopic "Pride of the Yankees."

Autograph of Gary Cooper, Hollywood, 1938. Cooper would portray the ill-fated Lou Gehrig in the classic baseball biopic "Pride of the Yankees" only a few years later.

Promotional still from "Pride of the Yankees" with Gary Cooper as Lou Gehrig and the real Babe Ruth (as himself of course).

Returning to the Bronx after a few months at liberty in Hollywood and its environs, Arthur settled down to work until World War II summoned him into the Army. Married before he shipped overseas (into the Pacific Theater of Operations), he spent his wedding night at the Concourse Plaza Hotel where he used to deliver those hand laundered shirts to Mr. Lee's customer. After the war, raising a family and building a business left little time for attending baseball games or collecting autographs.

Then, as word came that the venerated and venerable Yankee Stadium – the House that Ruth Built – was going to be torn down and a new Yankee Stadium would be erected across the street, my brother and I determined it was time to get Dad back to Yankee Stadium. The plans for the three of us to catch a game soon morphed into a family outing that included my brother's four sons who had never been to the Stadium. *Now age 87, it had been 71-years since Dad's last visit to the Stadium.*

RETURN TO YANKEE STADIUM: After 71 years away, Arthur returned in 2007 to the House that Ruth Built and visited Monument Park with some family members in tow. From Left: the then 87 year-old Arthur; grandson Eric; eldest son Fred; grandsons David and Gregory; daughter-in-law Karen, and eldest grandson Stephen. Photo by Richard Altman

We came early for the game with Oakland on June 30, 2007 so that we could tour Monument Park, see the batting practice and hopefully see the Yankees win. Monument Park was... *monumental.* There were the stone tributes to Ruth and Gehrig and DiMaggio and Mantle...the plaques for Jake Ruppert and commemorations of other great players and events from appearances by two Popes to a solemn remembrance of 9-11.

As we milled around our seats while Oakland took BP, someone on that team clocked a solid home run into the seats where we were standing. The ball came careening in, took one bounce and as it got airborne again, Dad reflexively put up his hand and came down with the ball. He did not seem surprised. My brother and I were astonished. His first trip back to the stadium since the 1936 World Series and he catches a batting practice homerun.

LOOK WHAT HE GOT...A batting practice homerun smashed by an unknown member of the visiting Oakland A's, ends up in the stands where our seats were located. In one, nonchalant, reflex action, it found its way into the hands of my 87-year old father. Standing with my brother Fred, Dad points out the scuffmark on the ball. Photo by Richard Altman

The ball bears a scuffmark either from where the bat struck it or where it impacted with the concrete before it bounced. It sits in a collectible ball holder at my brother's house…a gift from my Dad to his grandchildren. And it is inscribed, *"6/30/07 Yankee Stadium Caught by Grampa"* and it is signed on the sweet spot, *"A.Y. Altman."* Despite the fact that the Yankees lost to Oakland, it was a truly memorable day at the Stadium.

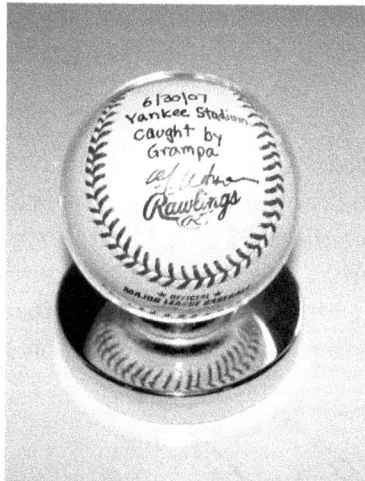

The Trophy Ball…The return visit to Yankee Stadium and "the catch" are forever commemorated with "sweet spot" inscription and signature…a gift from my Dad to his grandchildren.
Photo by Richard Altman

Postscript

It is April 2012 and I am fussing over syntax and putting the finishing touches on this epic tome before sending it to *Autograph Quarterly* for publication. The holidays are upon us and my Dad, Mom and brother are coming to celebrate with me. While they're here they'll have the chance to see some old friends too. The days go by quickly from their arrival on April 6th to their departure on April 10th when I drive them back home.

Minutes after returning home, Dad collapsed in my arms and was rushed by ambulance to the hospital. He was conscious and we talked during the next five hours as the doctors labored to determine what was causing his catastrophic decline. I tried to reassure him that everything would be OK and the doctors would fix what was wrong,

Then his blood pressure crashed and just like that, he was gone.

He was the greatest man I ever knew…my hero, my mentor, my friend and my Dad…and the loss is devastating. Just three weeks shy of his 92nd birthday and a few months shy of his 70th wedding anniversary and he's gone. We so wanted to celebrate both of those happy occasions…*and I really wanted him to read this story when it came out. I think he would have liked having his story told, especially to fellow autograph collectors.*

Love you Dad.

The Creation of The Declaration of Independence
By Stephen Koschal

During June of 1776, Thomas Jefferson participated in a Virginia delegation whose plan was to ask the Continental Congress to free itself from Great Britain. On the committee to draft a declaration of independence was Roger Sherman, Robert Livingston, John Adams and Benjamin Franklin. It was Thomas Jefferson who was assigned to write a declaration.

Jefferson needed a quiet place to concentrate away from the noise of downtown Philadelphia. He found furnished rooms in a fairly new brick house on the outskirts of the city. It seemed to be the perfect place to concentrate except for the numerous annoying houseflies from the stable across the street. The house was built and owned by a bricklayer named Jacob Graff. It was in this home that Thomas Jefferson wrote the Declaration of Independence in the course of less then three weeks.

Signature of Thomas Jefferson from the author's collection

During 1883, the structure was demolished. However, in 1975 the National Parks Service was able to rebuild the structure using old photographs. Jefferson wrote out a document which he called the "original rough draught." Some revisions were made by John Adams and Benjamin Franklin.

Signature of John Adams from the author's collection

The final draft had forty-seven changes. Added was an additional three paragraphs before the completed version was presented to Congress on June 28, 1776. Congress voted for independence on July 2 and continued to make changes to the document. When the Declaration of Independence was adopted on July 4th, thirty-nine additional revisions were made, some additions, some deletions. It appears most of the revisions were all made by Jefferson's hand.

It was time to have this document published. Late in the day of July 4, 1776 a Philadelphia printer by the name of John Dunlap was ordered by John Hancock to print the first copies of the Declaration of Independence. About 200 of these broadsides were published and they are presently known as the "Dunlap broadsides." These were the first published versions of the Declaration of Independence. Today, it is estimated that only two dozen of these original broadsides exist. A copy of this broadside sold at auction just a few years ago for a record price of over eight million dollars.

It was the very next day, July 5 that the president of the Continental Congress, John Hancock started to distribute copies of the broadside to many of the military and political leaders of our country.

George Washington had his personal copy read before some of the American army in New York. About ten days later on July 19, Congress ordered the printing of an official copy of the Declaration of Independence. This copy was to be signed by members of the Continental Congress even including some who had not voted for its adoption. They began to sign this historical document on August 2, 1776. Benjamin Franklin at seventy years old was the oldest member to sign the Declaration.

Eventually fifty six men signed the Declaration of Independence. I asked several autograph experts who specialize in autographs of the signers or other people associated with the Declaration, who do they feel top their list of the most interesting?

There was a wide range of names and mostly of those you would expect to hear. John Hancock, Thomas Jefferson, Benjamin Franklin, John Adams, Thomas Lynch Jr., Button Gwinnett and John Dunlap were the names mentioned time after time.

Signatures of John Hancock and Benjamin Franklin from the author's collection

Signatures of Thomas Lynch, Jr. and Button Gwinnett from the Koschal Autograph Reference Library

The signatures of Lynch and Gwinnett are some of the rarest signatures of all the signers of the Declaration of Independence. I would estimate that half of the signatures of these two that were offered by dealers and auction houses in the past were forgeries. Some of the signatures came with impressive certificates of authentication from high profile sellers of high end autographs.

The document illustrated below was offered to me at a Florida Book show during the 1990's. The person selling this item drove fourteen hours from Atlanta to show me this item. The asking price was only $100,000. To me it was instantly seen as a very poor quality forged document. The paper was right, the authentication was wonderful. The authentication was written at the bottom of the document by most likely the best known autograph collector of his time. His name is Lyman C. Draper (1815-1891). Some modern day collectors may be familiar with his name. He is the author of An Essay on the Autographic Collections of the Signers of the Declaration of Independence and of the Constitution (1889) of which this author is proud to have an inscribed and signed copy in my reference library.

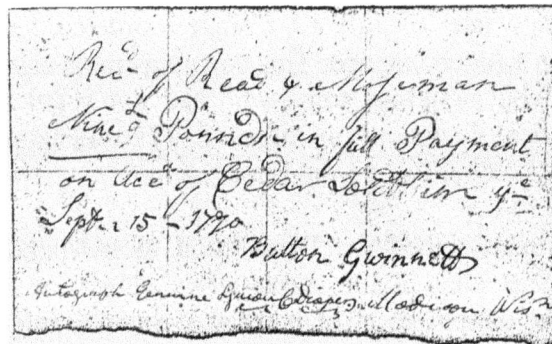

Forged document and signature of Button Gwinnett

Not only was the writing and signature of Button Gwinnett forged, I determined so was the authentication a forgery. There's a very good lesson to be learned here with regard to authentication. Of course, as usual, when owner's of items of this ilk are told their piece is not genuine, they rarely believe you. I hate to think that seller eventually found someone they would convince could have a good deal.

Two of my personal favorite names associated with the Declaration of Independence are John Dunlop and Mary Katherine Goddard. John Dunlap (1747-1812) was one of the most successful printers of his era. Born in Ireland, he moved to the United States and bought the printing business run by his uncle William Dunlap. John printed sermons and handbills. In 1771 he began the publication of the Pennsylvania Advertiser, a weekly newspaper. He joined the Revolutionary War and was an officer in the First Troop of the Philadelphia City Cavalry. Dunlap saw action during the battles of Trenton and Princeton with George Washington. Dunlap was also successful in printing currency. Illustrated below is a Three Pence note printed by Dunlap just one year after printing the Declaration.

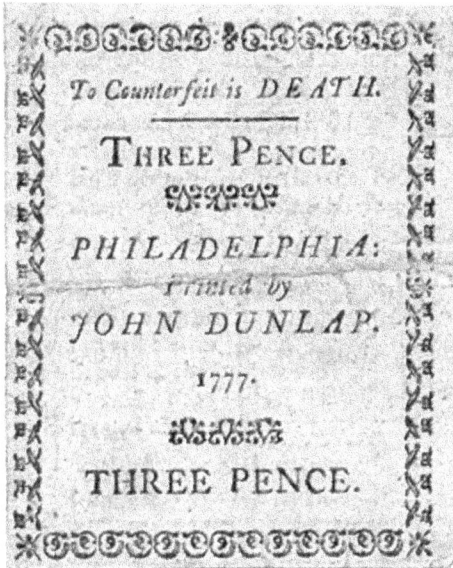

Three Pence note printed in 1777 by John Dunlap

Signature of John Dunlap from the Koschal
Autograph Reference Library

Signatures of John Dunlop are somewhat available and can sell for a fraction of the price of some of the rarer signatures associated with the Declaration of Independence. Mary Katherine Goddard (1738-1816) was an early American bookseller, postmistress and publisher. She was born in Connecticut. The Goddard family set up a printing press and were the publisher's of the Providence Gazette, the town's first newspaper. During 1775 she became Postmaster of the Baltimore Post Office becoming the first American postmistress. In addition she also ran a bookstore.

The Continental Congress decided that the Declaration of Independence needed to be distributed to all the states. Mary Goddard offered to print the Declaration knowing well of the risks of doing so. Many believed that doing so was associating yourself with promoting a document considered treasonable by the British. The copies Mary Goddard printed are known as "Goddard Broadsides." Although this was the second printing of the Declaration of Independence, it was the first to contain in typeset the names of those who signed the original document.

Uncommon signature of Mary Goddard from the Koschal Autograph Reference Library

Few autographs of Mary Katherine Goddard have come into the autograph market. Each one can be considered a historical treasure and a welcome addition to any collector who collects names associated with America's Declaration of Independence.

During 1820, there was concern about the condition of the original Declaration of Independence. The result was an Act of Congress to reproduce the document. During this time, John Quincy Adams was the Secretary of State. He commissioned William J. Stone, an engraver residing in Washington to reproduce the document. Stone did so by engraving a copperplate facsimile created from the original Declaration. The project was completed in 1823 and it was found that the Stone facsimile was quite an accurate copy of the original. It is believed the original printing by Stone was 201 copies made on vellum parchment. Each is distinguished by the words "Engraved by W.J. Stone for the Department of State, by order" printed in the upper left corner of the document.

Besides the vellum copies, Stone also produced an unknown amount of copies on paper. Autographs of William J. Stone can be considered very rare. Not one example of his signature could be found to be used as an illustration in this article.

Twenty years later, in 1843, Peter Force was commissioned by Congress to print books that became well known as *American Archives*. The set of books consisted of nine volumes. The original W.J. Stone engraved plate was removed from storage and used to produce copies of the Declaration of Independence on rice paper. The Declaration of Independence was folded and inserted into Volume One of the 5th Series of the Archives. The rice paper copies have printed in the lower left corner "W.J. Stone S.C. Wash." It is estimated that less then 1,000 copies were eventually printed.

Of all the signatures relating to the Declaration of Independence, two stand out as extremely eye appealing. One is of John Hancock and the other is of Peter Force. A signature of Peter Force is illustrated below.

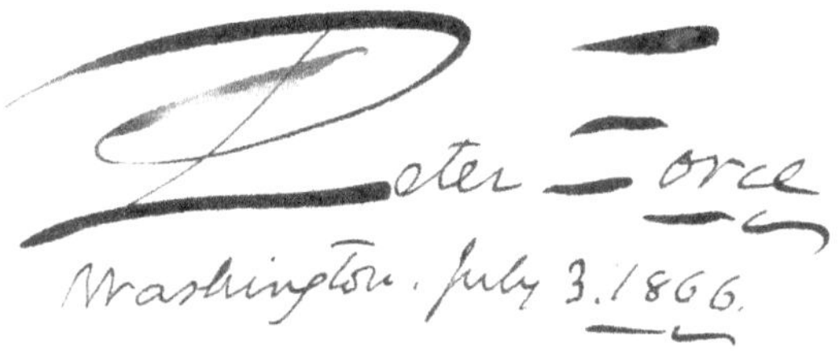

Signature of Peter Force, from the author's collection

Collecting signatures of those associated with the Declaration of Independence is an exciting and worthwhile venture. They are without a doubt the cornerstone of any collection of Americana.

Will the Real Jefferson Davis Stand Up?
By Brian M. Green

Jefferson Finis Davis, the first and only President of the Confederate States of America, was born on June 3rd, 1808 in (Fairview) Christian Co., Kentucky. He was the 10th and last child from which originated his unusual middle name, Finis, which is Latin for end/finish. This is supposedly what his mother told his father regarding any more children.

His early years were spent in Louisiana and Mississippi. He attended Jefferson College in Washington, Mississippi (1818) and Transylvania University in Lexington, Kentucky (1821). Davis entered West Point (New York) in 1824 and graduated in 1828.

He took part in the Black Hawk War (1832) under Colonel (later General and President) Zachary Taylor and eventually married his daughter, Sarah Knox Taylor in 1835. While visiting Davis' older sister in Louisiana (West Feliciana Parish), both contracted malaria/yellow fever and Sarah died three months after the wedding on September 9th, 1835.

Davis returned to Mississippi and built Briarfield plantation (Davis Bend, Warren County). He met and then married Varina Howell on February 26th, 1845.

In November 1845, Davis was elected to the U.S. House of Representatives as M.C., Mississippi. When the Mexican-American War began he resigned his house seat in June of 1846 and raised the Mississippi Rifles (a regiment), become its colonel. Davis fought at the Battles of Monterrey and Buena Vista. He turned down a promotion as a militia Brigadier General by President Polk and was appointed by Miss Governor Albert G. Brown to fill out the U.S. Senate seat rendered vacant by the death of Jesse Speight in 1847. In January of 1848 Davis was elected to serve out the remainder of the term. He was made Chairman of the Committee on Military Affairs. He was re-elected to the same seat but resigned to run for Governor of Mississippi in 1852. Davis lost by 999 votes.

In 1853 he was appointed Secretary of War by President Pierce. *Figure 3* shows his signature in this capacity. Note the characteristics of some of the letters, especially the "f"s, and "D" and "s" of Davis. He also briefly served as Acting Secretary of Navy and *Figure 4* shows an example of that.

1853 signature as Secretary of War

Signature as Acting Secretary of the Navy

With the end of the Pierce term in 1857, Davis ran successfully for the Senate and re-entered it on March 4th, 1857. *Figure 5* illustrates his signature as a U.S. Senator. Note the characteristics of some of the latters, especially the "f"s, and "D" and "s" of Davis. His renewed service in the Senate was interrupted by an illness which threatened with the loss of his left eye (1858). It was in the form of a chronic, relapsing ocular inflammatory condition. At this point it is speculated that Varina Davis began emulating the signature of her husband when necessary due to his eye problem and workload.

1857 Signature as U.S. Senator

Davis believed each state was sovereign and had the right to secede from the Union. When Mississippi seceded on January 9th, 1861 after the election of Abraham Lincoln as President in 1860, Davis had expected this but waited until he received official notification. On January 21st, 1861, the day Davis called "the saddest day of my life," he delivered a farewell address in the U.S. Senate, resigned, and returned to Mississippi. On January 23rd, Governor John J. Pettus of Mississippi made Davis a Major General of the Army of Mississippi.

On February 8th, 1861 a constitutional formed in Montgomery, Alabama. Davis was elected as Provisional President on February 9th. He had wanted to serve as a general in the C.S.A. Army and not as a president, but accepted the role for which he had been chosen. *Figures 6-9* illustrate various autographs by him as President of the C.S.A. Again, note the characteristics of some of the letters, especially the "f"s and "D" and "s" of Davis.

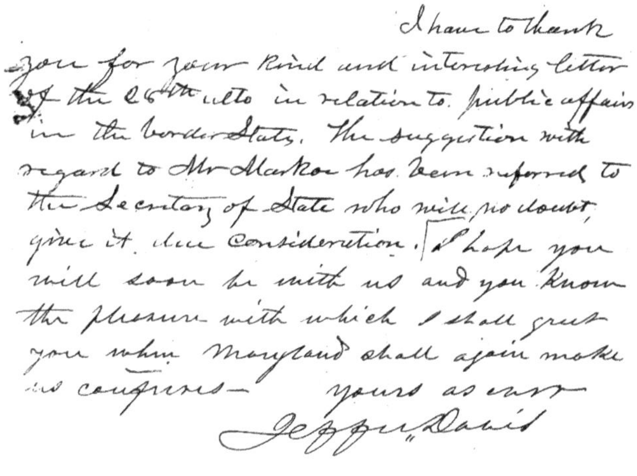

I have to thank you for your kind and interesting letter of the 26th ulto in relation to public affairs in the border States. The suggestion with regard to Mr Markoe has been referred to the Secretary of State who will no doubt, give it due consideration. I hope you will soon be with us and you know the pleasure with which I shall greet you when Maryland shall again make us confreres— yours as ever

Jeffer Davis

Signature as President of the Confederate States of America

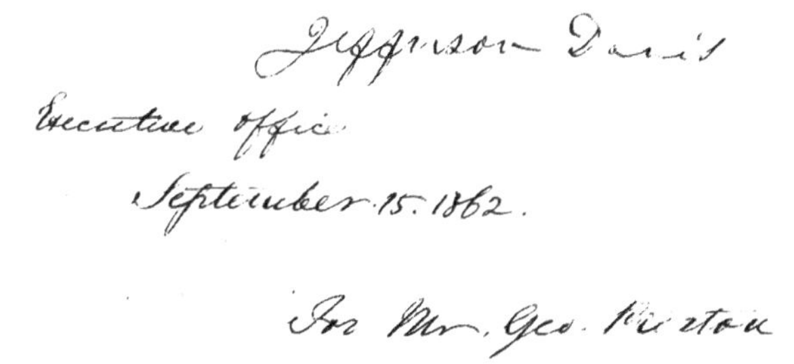

Jefferson Davis

Executive office

September 15. 1862.

For Mr. Geo. Kirton

Signature as President of the Confederate States of America

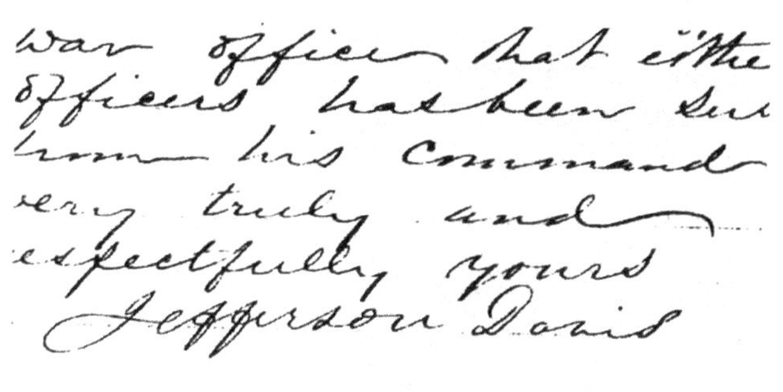

War office that is the officers had been sent from his command very truly and respectfully yours

Jefferson Davis

Signature as President of the Confederate States of America

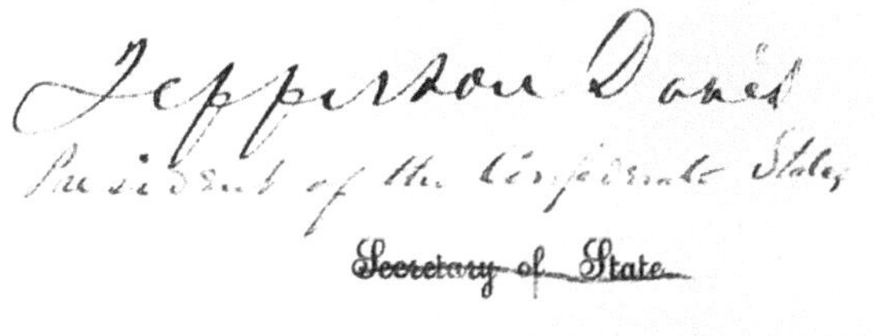

Jefferson Davis

President of the Confederate States,

Secretary of State

Signature as President of the Confederate States of America

Most historians sharply criticize Davis for his flawed military strategy, his election of friends for military commands and his neglect of the crises on the home front like the "Richmond Bread Riot" on April 2nd, 1863. Until very late in the war, he resisted efforts to appoint a General-in-

Chief, handling those duties himself. The appointment of General Robert E. Lee to that position on January 31st, 1865 was far too late.

After his capture at Irwinville, Georgia on May 10th, 1865, Davis spent two years imprisoned in a casement at Fortress Monroe on the Virginia coast near Hampton Roads (May 19th, 1865-May 8th, 1867). My last article in the December 2011 issue of A.Q. dealt with that aspect of his life. *Figures 10-12* show various examples of his handwriting during his imprisonment there. Again note the characteristics of the letters "f"s and "D" and "s" of Davis.

Signature while imprisoned at Fortress Monroe

Signature while imprisoned at Fortress Monroe

Signature while imprisoned at Fortress Monroe

After his release from prison, Davis visited Canada, Cuba and Europe. *Figure 13* illustrates such a usage in the form of an A.N.S. (autograph noted signed), signed in Canada on July 15th, 1868. He later became President of the Carolina Life Insurance Company of Memphis, Tennessee.

I have the honor to
be very truly yours
Jeffn. Davis
Canada
15th July 1868

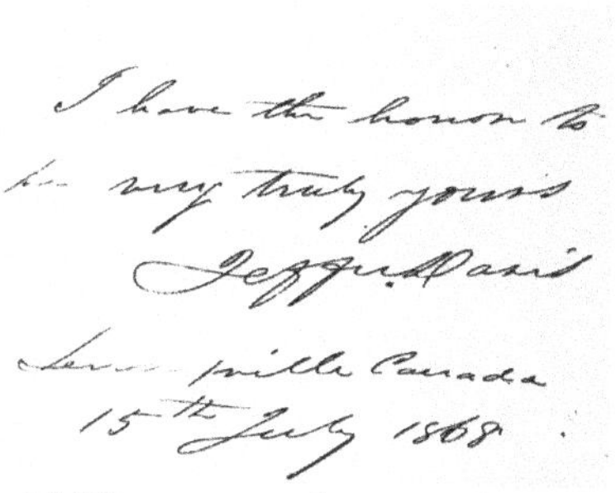

1868 autograph note signed

In 1878, Jefferson Davis returned to his home at Beauvoir, Mississippi on the Gulf. Over the next three years there he wrote his monumental work "The Rise and Fall of the Confederate Government." During this period and afterwards, the amount of correspondence became voluminous and Varina Davis frequently not only signed his letters (usually with a period), but wrote them as well. Even his checks were not immune. *Figures 14-19* show examples of this type of autographic material. *Figure 14* shows the signature portion of a letter signed by her as him but without the period.

With best wishes for you and
yours I am
Very respectfully
Jefferson Davis

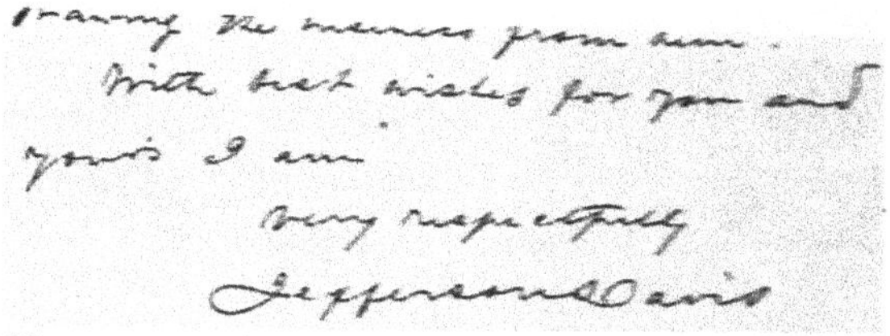

Jefferson Davis signature signed by wife Varina

Figure 15 illustrates a letter written and signed by Varina Davis as her husband on April 19th, 1886. Note the docketing on the cover/envelope reading "Jefferson Davis" which shows that the recipient (Captain Newell) thought it was written by Jefferson Davis himself.

Beauvoir Miss
19th April 1886

Capt. I. D. S. Newell.
Dear Sir.
Your note appended to the letter of Mr R. L. Thompson came here during my absence from home, hence the delay in this acknowledgement.
I do not know where the gate is, nor how far it concerns me. If it is for Limerick and your recommendation means that I should pay one half the license for the benefit of Limerick, I accept your proposition to pay the amt.
Respectfully & truly
yours &c.
Jefferson Davis.

Jefferson Davis
Capt. I. D. S. Newell,
St Joseph,
Tensas Parish
La.

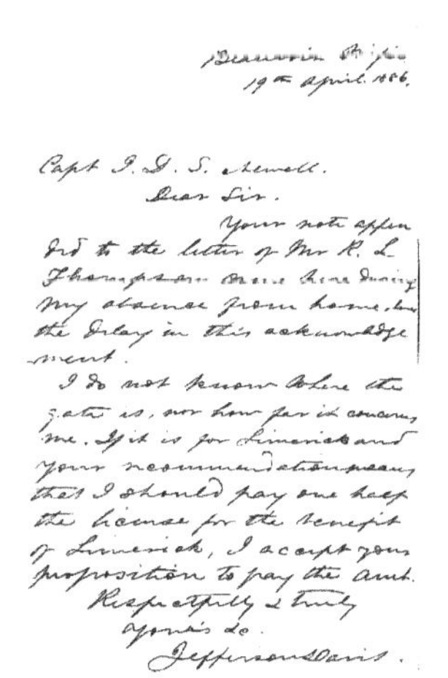

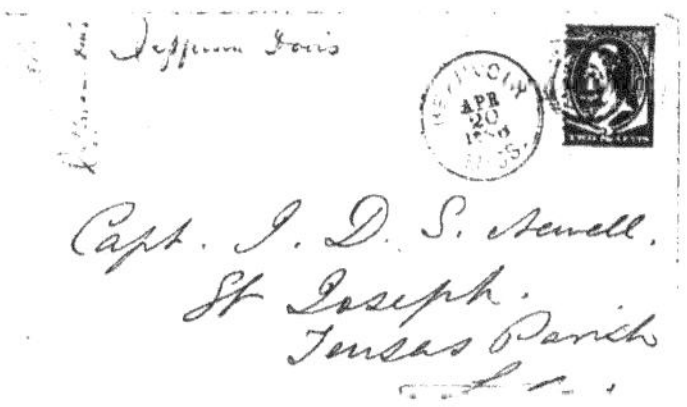

Figure 16 depicts Varina's version of his autograph as does *Figure 17*.

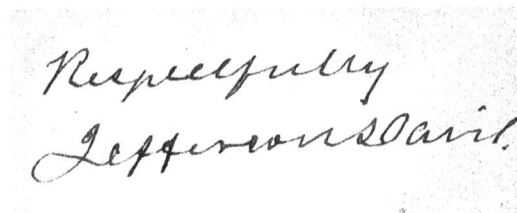

Note the characteristics of some of the letters, especially the "f"s and the "D" and "s" of Davis. The loop of the "D" is much closer/tighter in his than in Varina's. Hers is more circular and open at the top. His "s" in Davis on occasion looks like a Figure 8 whereas hers is more triangular. Davis makes the bottoms of his "f"s closer together than Varinas'. His writing is much tighter and more compact and legible than hers which has a softer touch.

More often than not, she placed a period after Davis (i.e. Davis.) See *Figure 15* for such a usage. Notice the wide spacing between "Davis" and the period. This makes it easy to delete by trimming it away as can happen (discussed later in this article). This period, according to many experts, denotes those signatures that were done by her for her husband. There are some who think her husband had done this on rare occasion for emphasis, but this author has never seen an irrefutable example of such. All seen by me were done by Varina Davis.

I remember selling a letter done by Varina for her husband in which his signature had the distinctive period. The next time I saw it (2 years later at a Civil War Show), the right hand margin of the letter had been trimmed away, removing the period. It was now being sold as a Jefferson Davis letter and not as one done by Varina for him. Chicanery at its best.

I have also seen letters written by Varina after her husbands' death (December 6th, 1889) in which she wrote that she had often written and signed his letters as well as his checks. *Figures 18 and 19* illustrate such examples. The first is from Rhode Island. In it she writes that "I have no signatures in my husbands' hand. He always dictated to me and as I wrote exactly like him and made facsimiles of his hand on checks etc., there are but few of his signatures now extant."

The second letter is from New York City. Here she mentions that she is sorry to not be able to send the lady "one of my husbands' autographs as he very seldom wrote even his name for fourteen or fifteen years of his life. My hand was so like his that I signed his letters and checks, and all of his business letters."

Figure 20 shows a variant of her post Jefferson Davis correspondence in the form of (Mrs.) Jefferson Davis dated January 20th, 1897 from New York City.

I have even seen a letter written by Jefferson Davis in which he said that even he had difficulty in telling which Davis wrote and signed letters and checks. Thus, if he had difficulty, think of the "outside of the (Davis) family collector."

For a long time, I (along with other dealers) thought the signed checks were above suspicion. Now, even they have to be carefully scrutinized. A letter by Varina I once had, discussing her writing/signing his checks, was sought after by another dealer so it could be destroyed. Needless to say, this did not happen.

Thus it can be seen how important it is to ascertain just whose autograph one is buying. It boils down to "Will the real Jefferson Davis please stand up?"

Jefferson Davis died in New Orleans, Louisiana on December 6th, 1889. Varina Davis continued writing and adopted his name "Jefferson". She would then sign letters V/Varina Jefferson Davis. See *Figures 18 and 19* for such examples. She died in New York City (where she was pursuing a literary career) on October 16th, 1906. No other political figure had such a wife who so effectively served as his private secretary (in the correspondence field).

Communist Leaders of China
By Dr. Zoltán Márián

China is a difficult country as far as autographs are concerned. You have to work hard if you want to receive a positive answer. After many years, finally I have received all the leaders' signed photographs.

Hua Guofeng /1921-2008/
Mao Zedong' successor as Chairman of the Communist Party /1976-1981/
Prime Minister of People's Republic of China /1976-1980/

Hua brought the Great Cultural Revolution / 1966-1976 / to close and prepared China for the process of economic reform. In the late 1930s, he joined the anti-Japanese guerrilla forces. In 1940, Hua had become propaganda chief of the county. In 1949, he joined the People's Liberation Army. By the early 1970s, Hua had not only become both first secretary of the Hunan provincial Party Committee and political commissar of the Canton military region, he had also joined the Party Central Committee. When Premier Zhou Enlai died in January 1976, Hua was his replacement. In the following months, with Mao's health deteriorating rapidly, a scramble for power started between Jiang Qing and her Gang of Four on the one hand, and Hua and his supporters on the other. In the end, Hua emerged victorious. On October 6, 1976, within a month after Mao's death, Hua had the Gang of Four arrested.

In power he instituted the policy of the Four Modernizations (agriculture, industry, science-technology, and national defence) which were intended to transform China into a powerful modern state. In 1979, Hua went on a European tour, the first of its kind for a Chinese leader after 1949. He travelled to West Germany , France and Great Britain. He also visited the Shah of Iran. Although China was a communist country, they had an ideological debate with the Soviet Union. When Yugoslavian President Josip Broz Tito died in 1980, both Hua and Soviet leader Brezhnev took part at the funeral. Hua and Breznev had a bad and hostile contact. Hungary and the other communist countries hoped that Hua and Breznev would make the first step towards starting a good relationship between China and the Soviet Union, nevertheless when Hua met several Statesmen in Beograd, he did not want to talk with Brezhnev. At that time Hungary was also a communist country and friend of the Soviet Union, so Hua was not popular here either. In 1980 Hua was replaced by Zhao Ziyang as Premier and he only remained as a member of the Central Committee of the Communist Party. He died during the Beijing Olympics so his death was not given much attention on the Chinese media.

Chinese leaders did not give out their signed photos. When I wrote Hua the first time, they answered me "giving autographs it is not in practice in China". Later on, I sent a photo to Hua asking him to sign it and Hua did it.

Zhao Ziyang /1919-2005/
Prime Minister of People's Republic of China
/1980-1987/
Leader of the Communist Party /1987-1989/

Zhao joined the Communist Party in 1938. In 1973 he was elected as a member of the Central Committee. Zhao was considered as one of the most reform-minded leaders in the 1980s. Zhao focused on economic reforms during the early 1980s. He also promoted a number of political reforms. The reform included proposals to have candidates directly elected to the Politburo, more elections with more than one candidate, more government transparency, more consultation with the public on policy. His economic reform policies and sympathies to student demonstrators during the Tiananmen Square protests of 1989 placed him at odds with some members of the party leadership, namely Premier Li Peng. The Tiananmen protests evolved into nationwide protests supporting political reform and demanding an end to Party corruption. Zhao visited the students and talked with in a friendly them said: "You are not like us, we are already old..."

The speech would be Zhao's last public appearance. Weeks later, army tanks rolled through the streets of Beijing after party elders declared martial law and soldiers shot an untold number of citizens at Tiananmen Square.

After breaking ranks from the conservative wing of the Politburo, Zhao was stripped of his powers and spent the rest of his days under house arrest until his death in 2005 at age 85.

I had a small sized picture showing Zhao with British Prime Minister Margaret Thatcher. First I sent the picture to Thatcher and she signed it. After it I forwarded the photo to Beijing and Zhao Ziyang signed it also.

Deng Xiaoping /1904-1997/

Deng never held office as head of state, prime minister or communist party leader, but he was the most important political figure in China in 1981-1989. His highest office was as Chairman of the Chinese Communist Party Central Military Commission. Deng was an intelligent man. He was nicknamed "a living encyclopaedia". Chairman Mao Zedong pointed out Deng's abilities to Nikita Khrushchev /1894– 1971/ of the Soviet Union. Deng visited the Soviet Union several times in the 1950s and the 1960s, as he was closely involved in Chinese-Soviet relations and their dispute over the international communist movement.

Mao and Deng parted ways in the 1960s as they disagreed over the strategy of economic development and other policies. During the Cultural Revolution Deng and his family were exiled. In 1973 Deng was brought back to Beijing and was nominated vice-Prime Minister. In 1975 he was elevated in a vice Chairman of the Communist Party. In 1984 Deng and British

Prime Minister Margaret Thatcher signed the Hongkong Declaration. After Mao's death Deng's economic policies required opening China to the rest of the world. His strategy for achieving these aims of becoming a modern, industrial nation was the socialist market economy. In 1989 Deng resigned his official positions. He died in Beijing at his age 92.

I had a small sized black and white photo which was taken about his meeting with Margaret Thatcher in 1984. Thatcher signed the picture first and Deng also signed it in 1985.

Li Xiannian /1909-1992/
President of People's Republic of China /1983-1988/

Li joined to the Communist Party in 1927 and served as captain for the Chinese Red Army during the Long March. In 1954 he was appointed Minister of Finance. He also was deputy Prime Minister until 1967. During the Tiananmen Square democracy movement in 1989, Li gave strong support to Deng Xiaoping for the military suppression of the movement. He also worked with Deng in the mid-1970's in trying to resurrect the economy from the damage caused by the Cultural Revolution. He was appointed President at the age of 74. In 1984 Li met President Ronald Reagan during Reagan's visit to China. Next year Li visited the United States. It was the first time a Chinese President paid an official visit to America. In 1988 Li resigned from his position and died in 1992 at the age of 83.

During his presidential term I sent a photo to Li Xiannian and he signed and dated it.

Li Peng / 1928- /
Prime Minister of People's Republic of China /1988-1998 /

Li Peng's father was murdered by the Kuomington when Li was 3 years old. He became the adopted son of Zhou Enlai, /1898-1976/ Prime Minister of China.

He was educated in Moscow and became minister of the power industry in 1981.

He became Prime Minister in 1988. He declared martial law during the Tiananmen Square protests in 1989. Li was instrumental in the dismissal and arrest of Zhao Ziyang, the leader of the Communist Party. He favored greater central economic planning and slower economic growth. From 1998 to 2003 he was chairman of the National People's Congress.

Li is well-versed in Russian and has learned English all by himself. He also loves reading. Newspapers once published a photo of Li showing him mending his overcoat. He said he learned sewing in the 1940s when he lived together with children of many other revolutionary martyrs. In 2010, Li's autobiographical book " The Critical Moment " was published. Li Peng is married and has three children.

I sent a photo to him and he signed it on back side.

Jiang Zemin / 1926- /
General-Secretary of the Communist Party of China / 1989-2002 /
President of People's Republic of China / 1993-2003/

Jiang's father was an educated man and his grandfather was a well known painter. In 1955 he was sent to work to Moscow at an Automobile Factory. Returning to China he was appointed director in the Industrial Ministry. After 1985, Jiang's career improved greatly. In 1987 he entered the Central Committee of the Communist Party /Politburo/. He became leader of the Communist Party in June 1989, cementing his position as the protege of and heir apparent to Deng Xiaoping, and assumed full leadership upon Deng's 1997 death.

Under his leadership, China experienced substantial developmental growth with reforms, saw the peaceful return of Hong Kong from the United Kingdom and Macau from Portugal, and improved its relations with the outside world while the Communist Party maintained its tight control over the government. He was instrumental in opening and improving relations with the United States.

Jiang loves reading and devotes most of his spare time to reading the latest science books. He also loves to read Mark Twain. Wang Yeping, his wife, graduated from the Shanghai Foreign Languages Institute and used to be head of an electrical engineering research institute in Shanghai. The couple have two sons.

Jiang Zemin' signed photo is an important item for me as he does not normally comply with such kind of request.

Zhu Rongji /1928-/
Prime Minister of People's Republic of China /1998-2003/

He joined the Communist Party in 1949. He graduated from the prestigious Tsinghua University in 1951 where he majored in electrical engineering. Then he worked as deputy head for the Northeast China Department of Industry. He purged during the Cultural Revolution, so he was transferred to work at a May Seventh Cadre School. In 1991 he became Vice Premier of the State Council, that is Deputy Prime Minister.

As Prime Minister, Zhu has a reputation for being a strong, strict administrator. For his hard work ethic and general truthful and transparent attitude, he is generally considered one of the most popular Communist officials in China. Zhu has a good command of English. In his free time, he enjoys the Peking Opera. Zhu is a 18th generation descendent of Zhu Bian the 18th son of Hongwu Emperor, the founder of the Ming Dynasty. He is married, they have a son and a daughter.

He signed a photo for me in red ink. I like his special signature.

Wen Jiabao / 1942- /
Prime Minister of People's Republic of China /
2003- /

He joined the Communist Party in 1965. Graduated from the Beijing Institute of Geology, he is an engineer. In 1989 he became Director of the Policy and Law Research Office of the Ministry of Geology. From 1986 he was the director of the General Office of Central Committee of the Communist Party.

A very knowledgeable person, Wen has a solid command of political and economic theories and profound attainments in natural sciences. As Prime Minister, in diplomatic and foreign exchange activities, he has also left people a deep impression with his steady and prudent manner and being well-versed in world affairs. In August 2010, Wen was named "The Man of the People" by Newsweek. In October 2010, Wen Jiabao was a person selected on the TIME Magazine's cover that the title was "Wen's World". In 2011, Wen was ranked 14th in Forbes Magazine's List of The World's Most Powerful People. He is married, they have a son and a daughter.

Wen Jiabao visited Hungary last June. I was lucky to forward my letter and photo to him in Budapest, and he signed and returned the picture.

Hu Jintao /1942- /
General-Secretary of the Communist Party of China / 2002-
President of People's Republic of China / 2003-

An exceptionally bright and diligent student, Hu attended the prestigious Qinghua University in Beijing, where he studied hydroelectric engineering. Hu is said to have enjoyed ballroom dancing, singing, and table tennis in university. In 1964, he joined the Chinese Communist Party. During the Cultural Revolution, in 1968, Hu Jintao's father was arrested for "capitalist transgressions." He was publicly tortured in prison that he never recovered. At the 14th National Congress of the Communist Party of China, which met in 1992, the 49-year-old Hu was approved as one of seven members of the Politburo Standing Committee. He became Vice President of China in 1998. As President, Hu Jintao likes to tout his ideas of "Harmonious Society" and "Peaceful Rise." Hu has shown a fairly hard-line approach to liberalisation of the media. He has been very cautious with regards to the Internet, choosing to censor politically sensitive material to a degree more strict than the Jiang Zemin era. He is very intelligent, he has a photographic memory. Hu is married, they have two children.

To get a signed photo from Hu Jintao is very difficult. Finally a contact helped me, who forwarded my request directly to the President. His signed photo is an important item in my collection.

My Interview with Lance Henriksen
By Mark J. Gross

He's an actor with a face you have seen in scores of films and yes, you know him well! This is one of those guys about whom you always say "I've seen him in everything." Mr. Lance Henriksen is just that celebrity.

I was quite lucky to sit down and interview Lance Henriksen in late 2011. He allowed me almost 20 minutes and afterward signed quite a few items for me gratis. He had just come out with his own book called *Not Bad for a Human.* If you are a fan of his, you'll remember that he played the role as Bishop, the artificial person in the 1986 film Aliens, in which he used the line that is now his book's title.

Promotional photo of Lance from the Aliens film franchise. Courtesy of 20th Century Fox.

This is an actor that has been in the business since the 1970s. He loves to play roles in sci-fi and horror film genres, yet, I have seen him play the "heavy" in quite a few films as well. Some of the first films I actually saw him in were *Dog Day Afternoon* (1975), *Close Encounters of the Third Kind* (1977), *The Right Stuff* (1983), and *The Terminator* (1984).

Lance is a very fun, yet laid back gentleman. He had fun just chatting with people at his autograph table during the convention he was attending in my home town of Baltimore, Maryland. I went to the Monster Mania Convention late last year and got there early with my press pass. Low and behold, Lance was the only guest in the celebrity signing room setting up. I asked him about doing an interview and he told me to come back in two days (on Sunday), and he kept to his word!

What follows are excerpts from our conversation.

MG – What got you interested in becoming an actor?
LH – I think it started because I went to movies as a kid, and that fantasy world was very seductive. Then over the years, I decided I really, really wanted to do it.

MG – Do you enjoy playing that genre type role and/or the "bad-ass" type role?

LH – Well, I was a good guy in quite a few films, but I do like playing those memorable bad guy roles, because they are sort of radical, most of them, and I die well I guess.

MG – When you were younger; did you particularly enjoy genre films, like sci-fi and horror?
LH – Well, when I was younger, a lot of films were in black and white, but The Thing was the one that got me the most, with James Arness as the Thing. It was beautiful that movie, and it scared me so bad, the in New York, I walked on the yellow line in the middle of the road, cause I was afraid someone was going to jump out at me. But it moved me and was a good movie.
(When Lance commented about films in black and white, I said, "for me too." A lot of people watching this interview laughed at what we were saying here.)

MG – Okay, what would be some of your favorite films that you were in yourself?
LH – Probably Near Dark, Aliens, Pumpkinhead... You know, I've done about 200 movies, and the adventure of the thing is what I remember. Whether or not the movie is successful, or for what reason I did it, it's just the adventure of it.

MG – Please tell me about your book.
LH – It's is called Not Bad for a Human. It worked on it with a co-writer for about a year and a half. James Cameron directed the film Aliens, so I asked if I could use that line from the film for my book. He said he would be honored, so he gave me permission to use the line from my character "Bishop".

MG – Any favorite actors/actresses you really enjoyed working with?
LH – Kathy Baker, who played my wife in the movie Jennifer 8, and that was another film I played a good guy in, but I love all the women I work with. When I did the film Johnny Handsome with Ellen Barkin, she was so beautiful, so wild, and such a great actress, I was actually shy around her. And Jeanette Goldstein, she was great. But, I get along with women very well.

MG – So what do you enjoy doing when you're not working? Down time.
LH – When I'm not acting I make pottery. I know that sounds very dull, but I make huge platters, and I need the labor of it, you know, to get away from the mental and go physical.

MG – What advice would you give to aspiring people wanting to get into acting, or writing, now that you're an author yourself?
LH – Read my book!

Everyone standing around watching my interview with Lance was now quite the huge crowd, and from their reactions and laughter, I think Lance and I did a good interview! Being able to chat with an icon in this genre, and movie history, I was honored to have met and sat doing a one-on-one with Lance Henriksen.

As many times as Lance has played such a "bad-ass" character, I was not too frightened sitting so close to him and doing this interview. After all, I consider myself lucky to be fully unscathed while interviewing a guy who has been a vampire, evil wild man, "bad-ass" biker, and all sorts of crazy "what the hell is this guy going to do to me?" roles. Plus, he has come face to face with aliens, a Predator, Bigfoot, demons, and so many other creatures! But to me, to also be able to interview a man who has been such a benevolent android such as "Bishop" in Aliens, I felt calm doing this interview, knowing that I would not be harmed, especially be such a cool and down to Earth artificial person!

I thank Lance for a wonderful interview, and for allowing me to leave in peace, and not pieces. Just don't ask him to that knife trick on your hand, ha-ha… Now don't piss this guy off – go out and buy his book, *Not Bad for a Human*. You'll be glad you did!

Salvador Dali and Pablo Picasso
By Stephen Koschal

Salvador Dali was born in Figueres, Spain on May 14, 1904. He became a prominent surrealist painter who was highly imaginative. His eccentric behavior always grabbed public attention.

During the 1970's Dali and his wife spent much of their time in New York City staying at their lavish suite at the St. Regis Hotel. The hotel is just around the corner from Fifth Avenue on 55th Street.

It was in the lobby of this hotel where I first met Dali and his wife Gala. We

Salvador Dali signing his book *Dali De Gala* in Paris, France on December 10, 1962.
Image Courtesy of Gamma-Keystone Photos

had a most interesting conversation and it was at this first meeting that I discovered how to stay in touch with this genius. With all the excitement of sitting in the lobby with him, attracting the attention of passersby's, on that occasion, I never did ask him for an autograph. That was soon to change.

I learned from Dali his routine schedule. He appeared to be a creature of habit. Both Dali and Gala spent their winters in New York City. He went to lunch the same time every day and went to the same French restaurant. The restaurant was only a short distance away from his hotel. Dali and Gala and their security guard would walk down 55th Street to the restaurant each wearing full length fur coats.

Dali, walking down the street, lit up more than a Times Square advertising sign. His handlebar mustache, his walking stick and occasionally his purple cape were an attraction not to be missed. During several years of the 1970's I estimate I met Dali and spent time with him well over 100 times.

When returning from lunch, almost every day he would enter the small bookstore and newspaper stand that was part of the hotel. The store handled some of the books Dali wrote and illustrated. Each day Dali would sign several copies of his book and place them back on the shelf. The signed copies always sold for the dust jacket price of the book. This was one of New York's best kept secrets. I remember when his coffee table size book came out in 1973 *Les Diners de Gala*. Over the course of several months I think I must have purchased 60 signed copies.

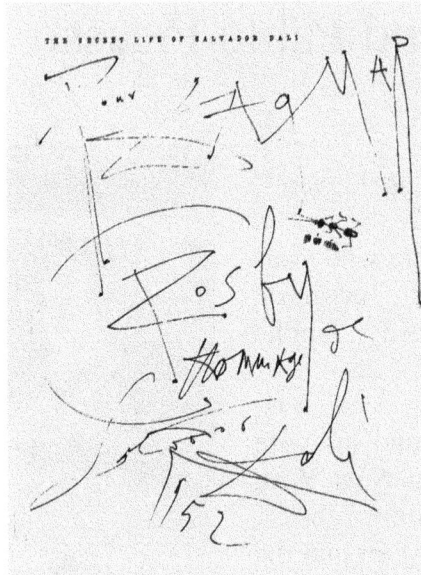

Vintage inscribed and signed book containing the scarce full signature of Dali
along with an original sketch of a black ant

Each time I met Dali, he was gracious to sign multiple items for me. In the beginning I started handing him books to sign then I graduated to posters of The Last Supper which I was able to purchase in volume from The Metropolitan Museum of Art Bookstore.

It took a few months before I handed Dali a photo of himself to sign. This is when I discovered he loved to look at pictures of himself. He did not sign that photo for me as he wanted it for himself. I course I obliged him. It was then I knew I had to find a source of photos.

Salvador Dali

That same day from 55th Street, I walked down to 42nd Street to the Daily News Building. Previously I purchased 8"x10" photos from this news company. One could go through their negatives and order prints for $5.00 each. I looked through their Dali files and ordered three photos. Later that week I went to meet Dali once again and took with me those three photos for him to sign. I was surprised when he wouldn't sign the photos but wanted the three as a gift. That day I didn't get any autographs but realized that every time I see him in the future I need two photos of each, one for Dali and one for me. That worked just fine until one day I handed him some photos, he went through them and took two and tore them up.

Apparently I pushed his wrong button. I handed him photographs of Dali being arrested in New York City. Years before, Dail was walking down Fifth Ave. and saw in a department store display a bathtub lined in fur. Dali picked up one of those very heavy New York corner metal garbage cans and threw it through the glass window of the store. He climbed into the display and was ripping the fur out of the bathtub. The photo I handed Dali was of him in the police station standing in front of the Police Sergeant's desk. The high desk was intimidating as it was much higher that Dali. When I ordered those photos it did cross my mind that he may not sign them but if he did they would be unique. It was worth the chance.

Salvador Dali caught the attention of forgers while he was still alive. I remember well, taking a walk with Dali up to Times Square. This area was filled with many tourist type stores selling electronics and a handful had limited edition signed prints by notable artists. I remember Dali banging on a glass store window infuriated. He told me "see that limited edition print in the window? That is not my signature, matter of fact it is not even one of my works." What forgers were doing is having prints made of works that would look like something Dali would do and forge the signature on 500 numbered prints." I have no doubt many of these apocryphal items landed in private collections.

When my inventory of Dali signed items became quite large, I took an ad accepting unsigned items from collectors and dealers. For a fee of only $25.00 plus return shipping I would get their items signed. For quite some time, many well known autograph dealers and collectors took advantage of that promotion.

During my friendship with Dali, I had two more experiences I wish did not happen. One of the photos I had made at the Daily News was a very attractive 8"x10" of the artist. It was a nice close up view of him elegantly dressed. As usual, one day I handed him the two photos and expected him to automatically sign one for me. Looking at the photo, he became outraged and tore those two photos into pieces. It took him a moment to get his composure. I thought this was the end of our relationship. I never saw him this mad. I asked him if he was alright and he apologized and started to explain. In the photo he was wearing a tiepin. While walking down the street one day, someone approached him, grabbed the tiepin and ran down the street. Apparently that photo brought back a bad memory of that theft. He told me one day someone even tried to grab his cane.

My last mistake with Dali came late in our relationship and just before he left New York to return to Europe. Dali's wife was always with him. He would lead the way and she and the bodyguard would be just a few steps behind. We were all walking together one day and I thought it would be nice to get a signature of Gala. Up to this point I had see her image on so many of his works but never a signature of Gala. While walking, I asked Dali if I could have his permission to ask Gala for her autograph. His hand and arms went flying like a mad man. "No, never he said. No, no, no!" At that point I realized how protective he was of her and certainly how scarce her autograph must be.

Gala was born in 1894 and she died in 1982. She was a mysterious woman, rarely saying a word. In 1912 she suffered a worsening of tuberculosis that had affected her for years. Her family sent her for care at the Clavadel Sanatorium in Switzerland. In 1929 Dali and Gala fell in love. They lived together for a few years and were married in 1934 in a civil ceremony. In 1958 they remarried in a Catholic Church. Gala served as a model in many of Dali's paintings. One of the most famous was her modeling as The Blessed Virgin Mary. It is said that Gala had a strong sex drive and had many extra marital affairs. One included her ex husband which Dali encouraged. Dali was a practitioner of candaulism. During the late 1970's she had a relationship with rock singer Jeff Fenholt who built his career upon his involvement with Jesus Christ Superstar and Black Sabbath. Gala gave him gifts of Dali's paintings and even bought him a million dollar home on Long Island.

During the 1980's Dali's health took a turn for the worse. His near senile wife was allegedly serving him dangerous cocktails of unprescribed medicine. Gala died on June 10, 1983 and Dali simply lost much of his will to live. He died several months later on January 23, 1983 of heart failure.

Signatures of Gala remain very scarce. They only place I know that you can occasionally find a genuine example are on some official documents. They are usually Loan Agreements which concern a loan of one of his paintings to a gallery or museum. Somewhat unique, these documents contain the scarce full signature "Salvador Dali" followed by the signature "Gala Dali".

Rare combination of signatures from a Loan Agreement

Knowing him for so long, my impression was Dali was autograph friendly and had a good heart. An interesting story is Dali drew a sketch of The Crucifixion and it was to be donated to the Rikers Island Jail in New York. For sixteen years it hung in the inmate dining room. For some reason, it was removed to the prison lobby for safekeeping. In March of 2000 it was stolen and has not been recovered.

PABLO PICASSO (1881-1973)

A Spanish artist and sculptor is regarded by many as the most influential artist of the 20th century. Although I never got to meet Picasso, I did have the opportunity of visiting his birthplace and home in Spain. His genuine autographs are not rare and can be found on many different types of items. His autographs can be found on cards, in books, prints and photographs. He is also available in autograph letters signed.

He went through periods of not signing for collectors but during the early 1960's for a short period of time, a collector could be lucky to get an item signed through the mail.

Typical Picasso signature received through the mail in 1960

Some collectors were lucky by sending Picasso a book and if requested they might get it signed along with a quick sketch.

Seems like that stopped for several years. Still, each year I would mail Picasso a color print from one of his books. Requests were ignored and the print would not be returned. It wasn't until around 1970 that he started to sign through the mail once again. From memory I think it took about three months to have it returned. Shortly after, I sent him a portrait of himself which he returned signed. Again, I tried my luck by sending him three portraits removed from his books to be signed. All three were returned signed. One was signed and dated. To my knowledge, no one else at the time was aware that Picasso started signing through the mail once again. Most of the items signed by Picasso for me were done so using a blue artists pencil.

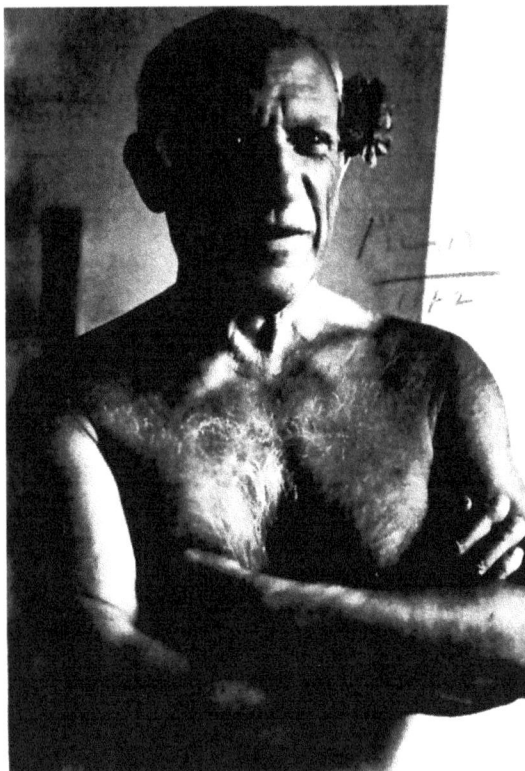

Print of Picasso signed through the mail 1972

Every few months I sent him three items at a time and this continued until the end of 1972.

The items I sent to him late in 1972 were never returned. On April 8, 1973 I learned Pablo Picasso died.

The Vice President of the U.S. Shot Me
by Patricia Claren

It was clear and sunny Saturday, February 11, 2006. The perfect day for a quail hunt. The incident would happen on the 50,000 acre ranch owned by Katharine Armstrong located in Kenedy County, Texas. Members of the hunting party included Vice President Dick Cheney, lawyer and Republican politician Harry Whittington, United States Ambassador to Switzerland and Liechtenstein Pamela Pitzer Willeford , the guide Oscar Medellin and Secret Service personnel. Katharine Armstrong and her sister, Sarita Storey Armstrong Hixon were in a vehicle at an unknown distance from the group.

According to the statement given by Dick Cheney the following incident occurred sometime between 5:30 PM and 6:30 PM. He claims that he was with Harry Whittington and Pamela Willeford shooting at a flock of birds. While Whittington was searching for a downed bird, Cheney, Willeford and Medellin walked toward another flock of birds about one hundred yards away. Whittington approached to within thirty to forty yards of the shooters. Apparently, a single bird flew up around and behind Cheney in the direction of Whittington. Richard Bruce "Dick" Cheney, the 46th Vice President under George Bush (2001-2009) had shot at the bird but had instead struck 78 year old Harry Whittington.

Dick Cheney hunting quail

Most of the damage from the shotgun blast was to the right side of his body including damage to his face, chest and neck. As usual, medical personnel and an ambulance that had been on standby because of Dick Cheney's well known heart problems. Fortunately they were now available to take Whittington to the nearby city of Kingsville before he was flown to Corpus Christi Memorial Hospital in Corpus Christi, Texas. He was admitted to the Intensive Care Unit in stable condition.

On February 14, 2006 some of the lead birdshot lodged in Whittington's heart caused a minor heart attack, atrial fibrillation, and a collapsed lung. Doctors did not plan to remove all the pellets from Whittington's body. They estimated that there were less than 150 or 200 pellets lodged in his body immediately after the shooting and about 30 pieces of shot will remain inside him for the rest of his life. Each pellet is less than one tenth of an inch in diameter. Whittington was released from the hospital on February 17, 2006.

Born March 3, 1927, Whittington is married and has four daughters and six grandchildren. After receiving his law degree from the University of Texas he began his practice in 1950. Over the years he has been very active in Texas politics. He has been on the many commissions including the Office of Patient Protection Executive Committee to ensure patient rights.

Harry Whittington

Mr. Whittington had only met Vice President Cheney three times over a thirty year period. They had never been hunting together prior to this incident. Mr. Whittington graciously apologized to Dick Cheney and his family for all the media attention surrounding the unfortunate incident. As late as October 2010 the Washington Post claimed that Cheney violated "two basic rules of hunting safety: he failed to ensure that he had a clear shot before firing and fired without being able to see blue sky beneath his target."

Mr. Whittington remains a very private person and his autograph is considered quite scarce.

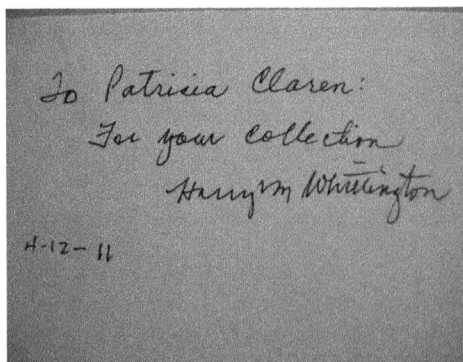
Autograph of Harry Whittington

Mr. Whittington has refused many media offers for interviews regarding his traumatic event that occurred five years ago.

Look...Back In the day...It's Superman

By Richard E. Altman

It's a comic book, a newspaper comic strip and the progenitor of the super-hero genre. It's also a radio show; several cartoon series; several novels; two movie serials; a live action TV series (actually *four* live action TV series); a Broadway musical and soon, a *seventh* feature film.

In about a year from now –June 14, 2013, if studio projections remain on track – the latest incarnation of Superman will debut on movie screens worldwide. Under the direction of Zach Snyder (whose previous helm-credits include "300" and "Watchmen") "The Man of Steel" stars English actor Henry Cavill (of "Immortals ' fame) in the title role and features a stellar supporting cast including Amy Adams as perennial love interest Lois Lane; Russell Crowe as our hero's Kryptonian birth-father; Kevin Costner and Diane Lane as the earthly step-parents Jonathan and Martha Kent, Laurence Fishburne as Daily Planet Editor Perry White, Christopher Meloni (late of "Law & Order SVU") as an American General and Michael Shannon as the Kryptonian super-baddy, General Zod.

Henry Cavill as Superman in "The Man of Steel" scheduled for release June 2013. Image courtesy of Warner Brothers.

As with other film and television interpretations, the iconic costume has been altered – presumably to fit both the actor and the times. Still, this film version presents the greatest departure of the film-costume design in the character's 75-year history. In its earliest rendition, the costume was far less stylized and far less consistent that it later became. The diamond shaped "S" shield was often a simply scrawled S inside of an inverted triangle, the iconic red boots were changed to yellow in one early comic adventure and the ability to "leap tall buildings in a single bound" was just that...flying came later as the character and his powers evolved.

The genesis of Superman begins in 1924 when a nine-year-old aspiring artist named Joe Shuster providentially moves with his family from their home in Toronto, Canada to Cleveland, Ohio. As grade school gives way to Junior High and then High School, Shuster meets an aspiring writer named Jerry Siegel and the two begin collaborating on various projects including one of the first sci-fi "*fanzines*." Debuting in 1933, their *mimeographed* publication was called "*Science Fiction: The Vanguard of Future Civilization.*"

In the third issue of that publication, Siegel, writing under the pen name Herbert S. Fine, tells of a villainous scientist who recruits a depression era vagrant from a breadline (this is 1933 after all) for experiments that turn him into a telepathic superman bent on world domination. In the end, subject turns on the master and kills him only to find that he cannot replicate the formula that gave him his powers. He ends up powerless and back on the breadline. The story was illustrated by Joe Shuster, with the villain bearing a striking resemblance to a future Superman staple, the evil scientist, Lex Luthor.

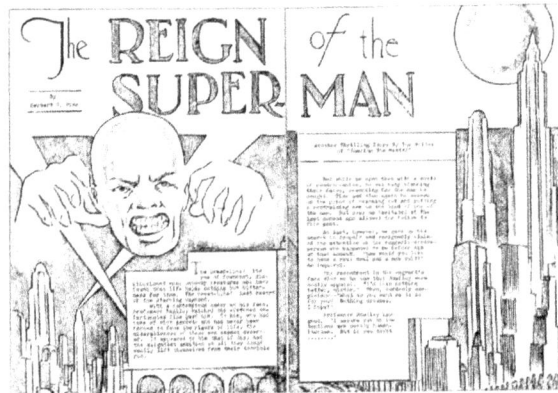

Double Splash Pages of "The Reign of the Superman" 1933.
Story by Herbert S. Fine (Jerry Siegel); Illustrations by Joe Shuster

The revelation for both Siegel and Shuster came when they abandoned the exploits of this Nietzsche-influenced Superman in favor of one who is a benefactor and protector of the human race. In this new take, an alien (illegal?) infant from another planet lands in the heartland of America and is raised as a human on a family farm in the town of Smallville. Now called Clark Kent, he appears to assimilate, all the while hiding his super powers. His parents raise him with the idealized American values to use his powers to help people all over the world.

Jerry Siegel and Joe Shuster at the drawing board

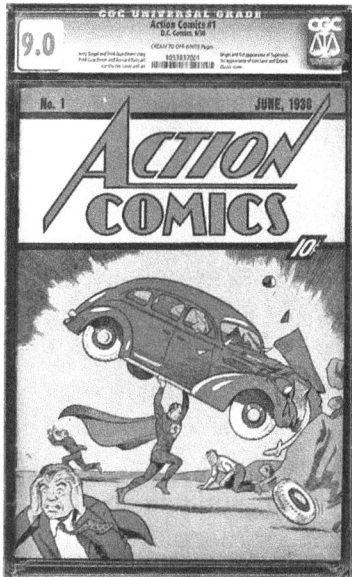

Action Comics No 1 (June, 1938)
The first appearance of Superman: This copy was sold at a December, 2011 auction by *ComicConnect.Com* for $2,161,000…*the most ever paid for a comic book.*
Image Courtesy of ComicConnect.Com

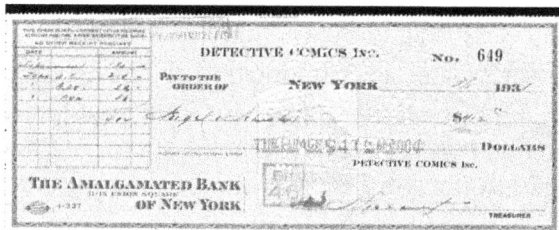

Check from Detective Comics made out to *Seigel and Schuster* (sic). As a result of misspelling both payees' names on the check, it was endorsed by Siegel and Shuster both incorrectly and correctly on the reverse. Note the memo section to the left for the line item that sells the rights to Superman for the sum of $130.
Image Courtesy of ComicConnect.Com

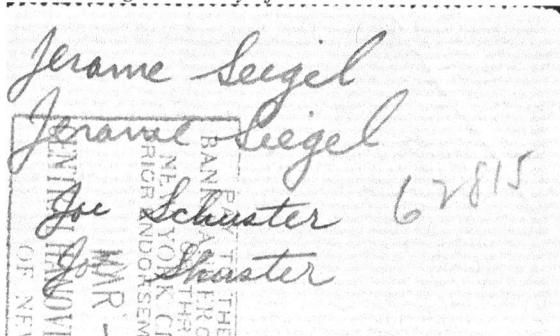

Detail of the Payee line
Image Courtesy of ComicConnect.Com

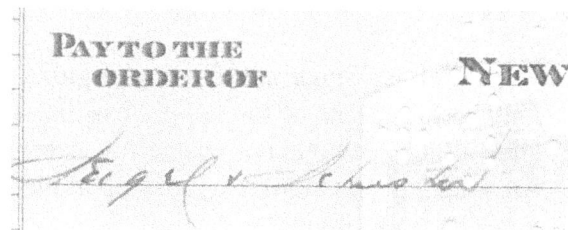

Detail of the dual endorsements
Image Courtesy of ComicConnect.Com

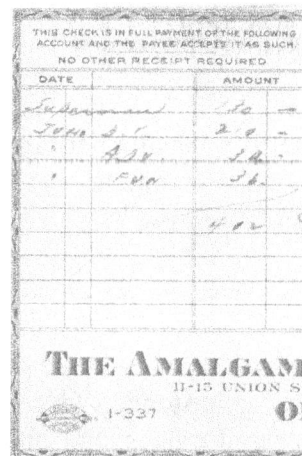

Detail of the memo section showing the sale of Superman for $130.
Image Courtesy of ComicConnect.Com

It is early December 1978 and I am working at the front desk reception area of the Loews Drake Hotel on Park Avenue and 56th Street in New York City. The night's arrivals include a block of rooms reserved by Warner Brothers for those associated with the soon to open "*Superman – The Movie*" starring a relative unknown with a familiar last name in the title role. Known primarily as a stage actor, Christopher Reeve dons the familiar blue, red and yellow costume to lead a cast that includes Marlon Brando, and Gene Hackman, His last name is initially confused by many who add an s to his last name, harking back to his Superman predecessor George Reeves who embodied the character for generations of fans in the 50s, and in reruns and DVD sets to this day.

An elderly couple approaches the front desk already lined with corporate executive types and present themselves for check-in. The man is a bespectacled Joe Shuster; the woman is his sister Jean. They are here as invited guests of Warner Brothers for the opening of the epic film spawned by his co-creation. Bad publicity in advance of the film's opening has motivated the company to compensate and honor both of Superman's creators, who unwittingly sold their rights to character to DC comics in 1938 for the sum of *$130*.

A lifelong Superman fan, I recognize Shuster's name and association if not his face and, breaking one of the hotel's cardinal rules against asking a guest for an autograph, I slide a piece of hotel note paper towards him while telling him how much I appreciate his work and his creation. He looks up at me, smiles at my words and then sees the proffered paper in front of him.

"*Would you like me to draw something for you?*" My response is one of astonishment at my good fortune. I had only intended to ask for an autograph. "*I would love that.*"

As he started – first with the ballpoint check-in pen and then quickly switching to a pencil – Joe Shuster drew a slashing diagonal line as he no doubt had done thousands of times. In short order, that line would provide the outline of the heroic chest of the "Man of Steel" in profile.

Though legally blind at this stage of his life – a fact I was unaware of at the time – Shuster deftly created a portrait of Superman in profile in a matter of a minute or two at most. As he was drawing his sister Jean told me that he normally would get $300 for such a sketch.

In those few moments, an amazing thing happened.

Virtually all activity at the front desk came to a halt. Those executive types that had been checking in stopped what they were doing and gathered around this man who at first blush appeared old beyond his years. They watched in silence as his again youthful hands recreated an icon of their childhood. They quickly knew that this was the man who co-created Superman all those years ago.

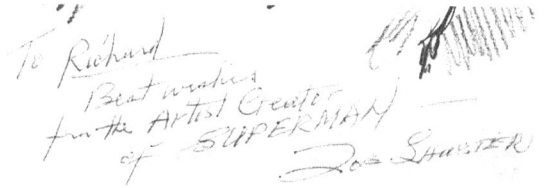

Detail of the inscription

Pencil portrait of Superman in profile drawn and inscribed by Joe Shuster at the front desk of Loews Drake Hotel, New York City, December 1978

As he finished the drawing, he inscribed it:

"To Richard
Best wishes from the Artist Creator of SUPERMAN –
Joe Shuster."

He slid the paper a few inches across the marble desktop to me and I began to thank him profusely for such a gift. He smiled and said, *"You know, I was afraid I wasn't going to like this trip. I think it's going to be alright."* Then he turned, took his sister's arm and was escorted to his guest room by the bellman.

Activity at the desk returned to normal and the corporate types returned home with an extra special story to tell about their trip to New York.

"You'll never guess who was checking in next to me at the hotel," it would no doubt begin.

Some might even ask, *"Didja get his autograph?"*

Far as I know, I'm the only one who did that day and it's been framed and hanging on my wall for the last 34 years.

Warner Brothers continued (and continues) to market Superman as one of its premier properties from generation to generation. Back in the '90s, the entertainment giant took a page out of Disney's book and opened a chain of retail stores. Among their leading product lines were all things Superman, from tee shirts to golf tees. Beyond the retro-kitsch Kent farm milk bottles and collectible cookie jars were lines of commemorative plates, statues and lithos, many at fine art prices. (We're not talking "The Scream" here but some giclées on canvas were priced north of $1,000 with many lithos in the $300 and up range).

While younger, rising stars in the comic art world like Alex Ross were among the most prolific and sought after suppliers of such art, in 1995 the folks at the Warner Brothers Studio Store did commission a print to commemorate the 60th anniversary of Superman. Entitled *"Jerry Siegel: Origins of Superman"* it depicted images from the first *Action Comics* and the first *Superman Comic* and was pencil signed by Jerry Siegel. The numbered issue was limited to 500 lithos and 50 artist proofs.

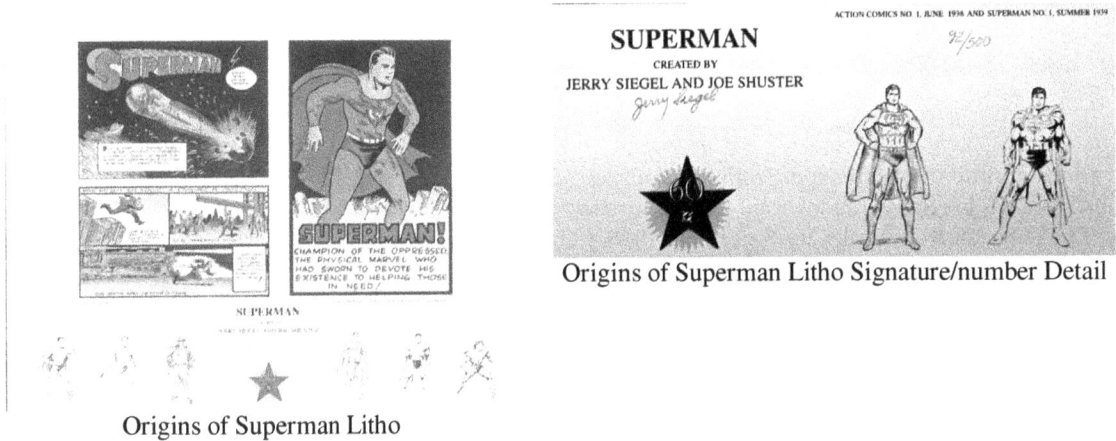

Origins of Superman Litho Signature/number Detail

Origins of Superman Litho

As the Superman industry grew so to did the character's back story, current powers and with them current perils. The brand extension as we would now call it, was impressive and damn near monolithic. Within a year of his debut in *Action Comics*, Superman began starring in an *additional* eponymous comic title. There were also animated cartoons, a popular radio show and ultimately an array of other comic titles in which the Man of Steel figured prominently. Practically every supporting character got his or her own book along with some new characters fashioned on the principal that imitation is the sincerest form of flattery (and the easiest way to make a buck, particularly when you already own the rights to the property your ripping…err…spinning off).

Siegel and Shuster Promotional Appearance at Movie Theater, date unknown. Based on the signage this presumably was a cross promotion with either the Superman animated cartoons or one of the live action serials starring Kirk Alyn.

Enter *World's Finest Comics* (pairing Superman with Batman and Robin); ("*Superboy, the Adventures of Superman When He Was A Boy*"; "*Superman's Girlfriend, Lois Lane*", and "*Superman's Pal Jimmy Olsen.*"

Sandwiched in between these decades of spin offs was one very important novel that actually altered the legend and lore of the character. Written by George Lowther and illustrated by Joe Shuster, "The Adventures of Superman" was first published in 1942. Lowther has the distinction of being the first credited author of a Superman story other than Jerry Siegel.

Lowther's tome gives us back story, revealing details of Superman's doomed birth-planet Krypton, changing his birth parent's names from Jor-L and Lora to Jor-El and Lara, before landing the tot of steel (and us) in Smallville, USA for the formative years with adoptive earth parents Eben and Sarah Kent. (They would not be renamed Jonathan and Martha Kent until 1952).

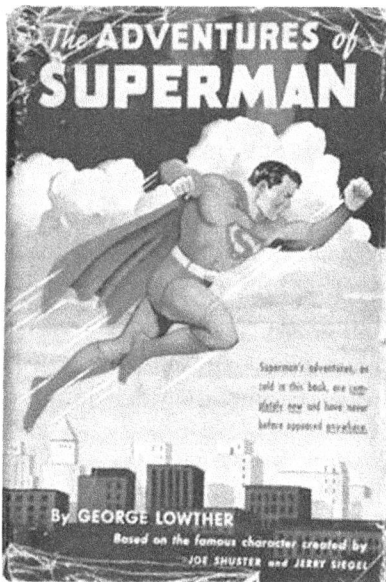

Cover of original 1942 edition of George Lowther's novel, The Adventures of Superman. Though it has been reissued several times in hardcover and trade paperback, the original edition remains a sought after collector's piece with prices governed by condition and demand.

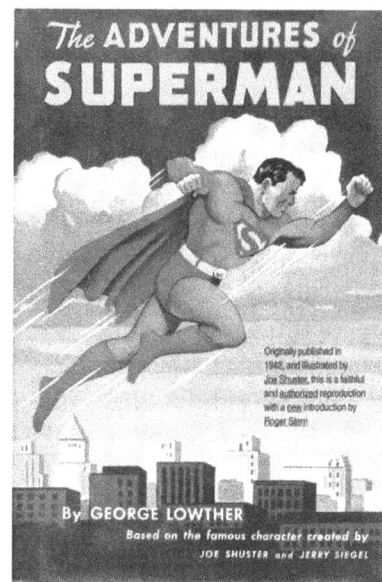

Cover of hardcover reprint 1995. Applewood Books

Lowther's book was the first novelization of a comic book character and it set the stage for what was to come both for Superman and the super hero comics industry. Lowther would also not be the last writer other than Siegel to be given Superman story credit. A couple of years before Applewood was issuing its hardcover reprint of Lowther's book, DC writer Louise Simonson (yes, a female superhero comic book writer) teamed up with DC veteran artists Dan Jurgens and José Luis García-López to do a Young Adult novelization of the "Death of Superman" storyline for the Bantam Books imprint. The title, "*Superman: Doomsday and Beyond*" has a major distinction to its credit. The cover art was created by up and coming (and now superstar) artist Alex Ross and was his very first commission for any DC character.

Cover of "Superman: Doomsday and Beyond"
signed by Alex Ross

Preliminary, original Superman study pencil sketch
for the cover of "Superman: Doomsday & Beyond"
signed by Alex Ross

Just across the river from scenic Paducah, Kentucky there is a Southern Illinois town named Metropolis. With a population of 6,500+, its name was clearly an expression of the (over) optimism of its founders. For the record, its name predates Siegel, Shuster and Superman…hell its name predates the iconic Fritz Lang silent movie. Having more in common with the rural "Smallville" than the urban power-center imagined in the comics, Metropolis, Illinois is located on the Ohio River and was platted back in 1839.

Among the attractions in Metropolis, Illinois is a Harrah's Casino, Fort Massac State Park, a town square that is presided over by a 15-foot bronze statue of Superman, an annual Superman celebration, and the Super Museum, owned and operated by Superman fan and formidable expert, Jim Hambrick. Arguably the foremost repository of all things Superman, the Super Museum features everything from movie costumes and props to green painted kryptonite rocks and vintage Superman memorabilia.

Officially the "Home of Superman" with the blessings of both Warner Brothers and the Illinois State Legislature, the town's *weekly* newspaper is the *Metropolis Planet*. A transplanted Californian, Jim Hambrick has been a driving force behind promoting and advancing the town's Superman connections.

For years before moving to Metropolis Hambrick ran his museum as a mobile attraction at State Fairs and the like, while working closely with many of those instrumental in making and sustaining the character over the years. Notably of course among them were Jerry Siegel and Joe Shuster and the screen's first live action Superman, Kirk Alyn.

Signed Publicity Photo of Kirk Alyn as Superman Reading a Superman Comic

Before George Reeves did cinematic battle with the forces of evil and ignorance who were attacking munchkins wielding an *Electrolux* death ray ("Superman and the Mole Men" Lippert Pictures 1951), serial star Kirk Alyn portrayed Superman in two 15-chapter Columbia movie serials: "Superman" (1948) and "Atom Man vs. Superman" (1950).

Working with all three of the then unheralded Superman veterans, Hambrick created a souvenir certificate that the now growing number of fans could purchase. Made to resemble a municipal citation, the fanciful "Superman of Metropolis Award" was signed by Kirk Alyn as Clark Kent, Joe Shuster as "President of the Metropolis Chamber of Commerce" and Jerry Siegel as "Mayor of the City of Metropolis."

Superman of Metropolis Award

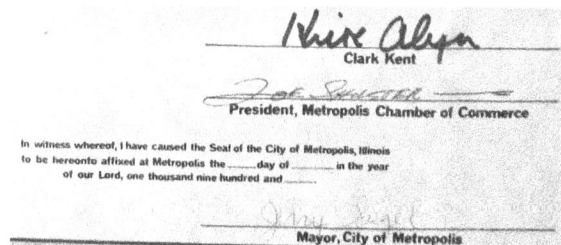

Superman of Metropolis Award Signature Detail

Scene from "Superman and the Mole Men" starring George Reeves
(L-R) Mole Men and former Munchkins Jerry Maren and John T. Banbury (holding the customized and deadly Electrolux/funnel combo); Mole Man Tony Baris. (*Not shown on account of being in the hospital after getting shot by the bad guys: Mole Man and former Munchkin Billy Curtis*)

In the three-quarters of a century since Superman was introduced to the world, the influence the character has wielded and the world-wide affection it has engendered is far beyond the imagination of even Jerry Siegel and Joe Shuster, who after all were mere "mortal men." The alien from another planet that came to represent "truth, justice and the American way," also helped raise war bond money to "fight the "*Japanazis*" in World War II; extolled the virtues of physical fitness and encouraged youngsters to exercise, and even helped UNICEF and NATO discourage curious youngsters in Bosnia-Herzegovina from picking up and playing with things found in former mine and battlefields. The comics were published in English as well as Cyrillic and Latin/Roman scripts for the Serbo-Croatian population.

Front Cover of the "Superman Deadly Legacy" in English.

Back Cover of the "Superman Deadly Legacy" in English

Back Cover of the "Superman Deadly Legacy" in
Cyrillic

Back Cover of the "Superman Deadly Legacy" in
Latin/Roman

*The more things change...*Note the similarity to the 1938 Joe Shuster artwork, dual signed in later life by
both Jerry Siegel and Joe Shuster
Courtesy of the Jim Hambrick Collection, Super Museum, Metropolis, Illinois

So too over the course of 75-years, a great many artists and writers have tried their hand at bringing "The Man of Steel" to the page, some with more popular success than others. The character has been retooled, reinvented and reintroduced to succeeding generations while keeping the core values intact. From those who worked directly with Siegel and Shuster in what has come to be called comic's "Golden Age" to the subsequent "Silver Age" and "Bronze Age" artists, Superman endures.

One standout artist that spanned all three of comic books' metallic ages was the legendary Curt Swan. He is revered by fans and fellow artists for the humanity and emotion he brought to his renditions, not just of Superman but to many characters in the extensive pantheon of DC super heroes. Swan's "pencils" remain among the most collectible to this day.

Complimenting his style as naturally as one could wish was master "inker" Murphy Anderson. Indeed the pair worked so well together for so many years that fans began referring the resulting artwork as a *"Swanderson."*

Growing up in the 50s and 60s – even though comic book artists were frequently uncredited – the work of Curt Swan stood out from the other artists plying their art in the by now myriad of Superman related titles on offer. Indeed in my young life, Swan's interpretation of Superman on paper was as definitive as George Reeve's portrayal was on the TV screen.

"Swanderson" Superman print, hand signed by the legendary art team of Curt Swan and inker Murphy Anderson

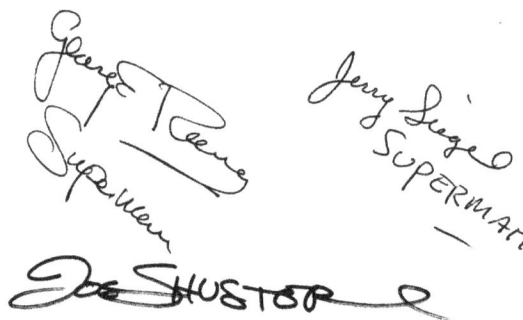

Autographs on a single card of George Reeves, Jerry Siegel and Joe Shuster. *Image courtesy of the Jim Hambrick Collection, Super Museum, Metropolis, Illinois*

Hastily drawn sketches of Superman by Jerry Siegel and Joe Shuster
Courtesy of the Jim Hambrick Collection, Super Museum, Metropolis, Illinois

Today, one of the most influential comic artists is a Chicago-based painter named Alex Ross. His realistic style has earned him favorable comparisons to Norman Rockwell and like Rockwell, Ross's painted panels have made him a favorite among cover artists.

Additionally, Ross's periodic forays into comic books not just on the cover but from cover-to-cover are much anticipated by fans. Ross tells stories with panels that are not drawn, inked and colored but entirely painted. In so doing, he has created some of the most memorable oversized comics and graphic novels in the last decade or more. It has also spawned a cottage industry for Alex Ross posters, lithos, plates, statues, tee shirts, trading cards and even action figure lines. His appearances at comic book stores and comic conventions – now increasingly rare – draw hundreds and even thousands of fans.

As much as his technique is a departure from the traditional comic book style and process, Alex Ross still brings a fan's love to the medium and it shows in his reinterpretations of some of the comic world's most enduring images. Without a doubt, the most frequent object of his homage artwork is Joe Shuster, *without whom (along with Jerry Siegel) an entire industry might not have been born.*

Joe Shuster's Early and Iconic Image of Superman
snapping chains with his chest

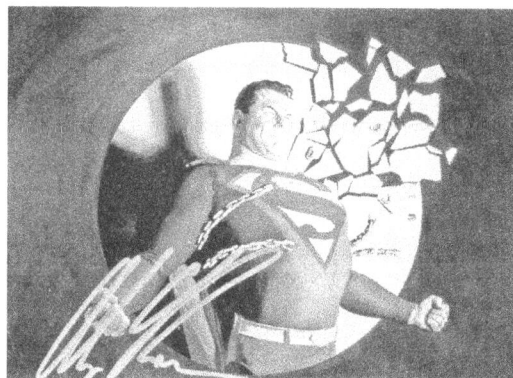

Alex Ross homage to Shuster's breaking chains
image, signed in silver sharpie.

Presidents of the United States Autopen Guide
By Stephen Koshal and Andreas Wiemer

Attempting to duplicate ones handwriting dates back to the early 1780s. Many contraptions were created for this purpose with names such as polygraph, pantograph, copying press, stylographic writer and mechanical writer, Signo, Tin Man, Robot Signer, Signa-Signer and several decades ago, the Autopen.

Much has been written since the mid-1960s about the Autopen in autograph reference books. Autograph authentication continues to be one of the major problems in the autograph industry. It's nearly impossible for a new collector to be able to determine whether a signature is genuine, stamped, printed, secretarial, or signed by the Autopen. Only some people with decades of experience and a large reference library are capable of knowing the difference. As it is, if a novice relies on what has been put in print they can become more confused.

Most autograph collectors realize that one of the most popular areas of collecting are items bearing the signatures of Presidents of the United States. In Charles Hamilton's book *The Robot That Helped To Make A President*, he states: "...no chief executive before JFK employed a robot to sign his name..." The authors of this book have clearly identified ten different Eisenhower Autopen patterns.

Because of the huge amount of correspondence the use of the Autopen actually became popular with Eisenhower. This educational study will focus on Eisenhower up to Barack Obama. Also, the authors will attempt to correct some erroneous information published elsewhere.

This Autopen reference study illustrates all the known and confirmed Autopen examples of the Presidents of the United States. There are illustrations in some other books said to be an Autopen example of a certain President. However, with extensive research by the authors of this book, those examples could not be confirmed, therefore they are not illustrated in this book.

This is the first time autograph collectors and dealers have one book on hand to compare their presidential signatures with Autopen examples. Presidents of the United States, Autopen Guide was made possible through International co-operation. Should readers have a confirmed Autopen example not found in this book, the authors would be pleased to hear from you. If confirmed, your example will be published in future editions. The entire hobby will always benefit when information is shared.

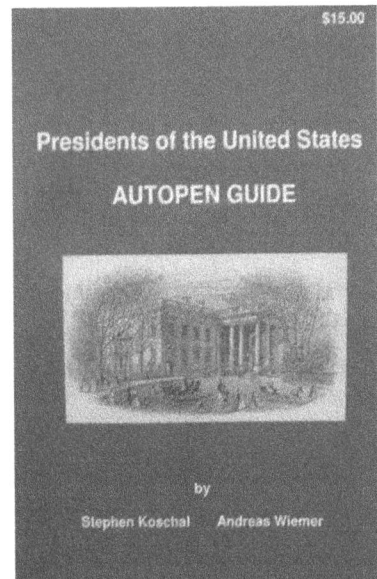

www.ingramcontent.com/pod-product-compliance
Lightning Source LLC
Chambersburg PA
CBHW080530030426
42337CB00023B/4686